ON THE
MEANING OF LIFE

by
Will Durant

edited by
John Little

Promethean Press
Dallas   Vancouver   Ontario

ON THE MEANING OF LIFE

Published by:
Promethean Press
1846 Rosemeade Parkway #192
Carrollton, TX 75007

ISBN 0-9737698-0-7

Manufactured in the United States of America

TABLE OF CONTENTS

INTRODUCTION

In the Fall of 1930 Will Durant found himself outside his home in Lake Hill, New York, raking leaves. It was typical weather for the time of year and the cold refreshing air blowing in from upstate had infused him with a sense of invigoration as he went about his task.

As Durant continued his raking, he was approached by a well-dressed man who told him in a quiet tone that he was going to kill himself unless the philosopher could give him a valid reason not to. Not having the time to wax philosophic on the matter, Durant did his best to furnish the man with reasons to continue his existence. As Durant would later recall:

> I bade him get a job - but he had one; to eat a good meal - but he was not hungry; he left visibly unmoved by my arguments. I do not know what happened to him. In that same year I received several letters announcing suicide; .... I learned later that there had been 284, 142 suicides in the United States between 1905 and 1930

What a dilemma - and what a statistic! And more recent statistics are even more alarming: The World Health Organization estimated that in the year 2000 alone, one million people took their own lives; in the United States, an average of 84.4 people per day commit suicide, resulting in 30,903 self-inflicted deaths per year. Every 17.1 minutes, one person gives up hope and ends their life.[1]

Is it any wonder, then, -- and can there be a more important question? -- that "What is the meaning of life?" is the perennial question of philosophy? Academics and sages have spent billions of collective brain cells over the centuries attempting to formulate a reply to this eternal query. For some, it is an intellectual mouse hunt, for others, as we've seen, the answer to this question holds very deep meaning - and potentially fatal consequences. The question itself implies many other questions; why are we here? Is there a God? If so, why do we suffer so much? If not, then what is the point of our existence? Is our existence on this planet merely a dress rehearsal for a better play to follow - or is this all that there is? And what is existence? -- Nothing more than a freak cosmological farce; a fortuitous congruence of atoms that, over millions of years, resulted in the creation of sentient beings - "full of sound and fury, signifying nothing?" Or is there some deeper meaning that can be fathomed? According to Durant, this problem of the meaning of life had long held particular significance to him:

> Ever since my loss of religious faith I had brooded over this prob-
> lem, and at times I had sunk into a mood of despondency akin to
> the angst or *angoisse* contemporaneously expressed by French
> and German existentialists... I proposed to sound out various
> notables on the meaning of life, to print their answers, and to add
> my own.[2]

Durant sat down and penned a letter; philosophical in its questions and poetic in its appeal. He sent it out to 100 individuals, challenging them to respond not only to the fundamental question of life's meaning (in the abstract) but also to relate how they each (in the particular) found meaning, purpose and fulfillment in their own lives. In Durant's words:

> ...what are the sources of your inspiration and your energy, what
> is the goal or motive-force of your toil, where you find your con-
> solations and your happiness, where, in the last resort, your
> treasure lies?

Surely, Durant hoped, the responses he received from such luminaries would contain something that would have sufficiently answered the question of that well-dressed stranger who appeared in his garden that autumn day in 1932. In fact, it did far more than this; the responses, rather than being dark and brooding, were instead uplifting and positive, expressing joyous exaltation at the very fact of existence along with personal insights on how to make life more meaningful. The responses came from all points of the compass and from a stellar list of notables: the great spiritual leader Mohandas K. Gandhi; the (then) Prime Minister of India, Jawaharlal Nehru; the American author/curmudgeon H.L. Menken; author and Naturalist Theodore Dreiser; Sinclair Lewis (the first American to win the Nobel Prize for Literature); novelist/professor (Columbia) John Erskine;

Charles A. Beard (perhaps the most influential historian in American history); the poet John Cowper Powys; Edwin Arlington Robinson (who, at one time, was considered the greatest poet in the United States); Dr. Charles Mayo (founder of the Mayo Clinic); the renowned Russian-American pianist and conductor Ossip Gabrilowitsch; the artic explorer/adventurer /author Vilhajalmur Stefansson; the randy English psychologist/author Havelock Ellis; Carl Laemmle (the founder of Universal Studios, Hollywood); Ernest M. Hopkins (former President of Dartmouth College); the great newspaper publisher Adolph S. Ochs (a man who acquired *The New York Times* in 1896 and later controlled the *Philadelphia Times* and the *Philadelphia Public Ledger* and a man who was known for stressing nonpartisan, almost clinical, news reporting); American clergyman/author John Haynes Holmes (who was a close friend of Mahatma Gandhi's and a founder of the National Association for the Advancement of Colored People as well as the American Civil Liberties Union); Admiral Byrd, humorist Will Rogers; Henry Fairfield Osborn (of the American Museum of Natural History); the French philosopher and novelist Andre Maurois; C. V. Raman (winner of the 1930 Nobel prize for physics); Abbe Dimnet, the philosopher/author of the best-selling *The Art of Thinking*; Mary Emma Woolley (renowned educator and former president of Mt. Holyoke College); Scientist/author Gina Lombroso; American athlete Helen Wills Moody (long considered by many as the greatest female tennis player in the history of the sport; winning a total of 19 singles titles at the French championships, Wimbledon and the United States championships); the great Irish playwright George Bernard Shaw; Nobel Prize winning philosopher Bertrand Russell; Count Hermann Keyserling (generally counted the first Western thinker to conceive and promote a planetary culture, beyond nationalism and cultural ethnocentrism, that was based on the recognition of the equal value and validity of non-Western cultures and philosophies). To round out the viewpoints, there was even a contribution from an inmate serving a life sentence in Sing Sing prison.

Most replies were substantial, others were terse (Keyserling) and dismissively evasive (George Bernard

Shaw and Bertrand Russell). In revisiting the book's contents in the late 1970s (some 40 years after having written it), Durant reflected:

> Looking over those replies today...I like best those of Beard, Powys, and Maurois. The most touching letter, however, came from Convict 79206...

Once all the replies were in, Durant took his turn; facing up to his own questions with a reply that is itself a work of high philosophy and empowering optimism. Durant entitled the book *On The Meaning Of Life* and it was released to the general public by a small publishing house in 1932. It was not promoted and found its way into few hands. Almost no copies of the original version of the book exist at present day. This is a terrible situation as, in many respects, it is the most important book in Durant's oeuvre. With the hope of rectifying this situation I have re-edited the manuscript and offer it once more for your consideration as *On The Meaning Of Life* is a powerful book on a very powerful topic and, particularly in light of the statistics cited above, a book that needs to remain in print and before the public as - at least - an alternative to darker thoughts.

In this book Will Durant has fashioned a true "dream team" of supporting players for his cast that are both profound and diverse; surely one of these people (if not Durant himself) has something to offer you that will help you in your life -- such a grouping of poets, philosophers, saints, inmates, athletes, Nobel Prize winners, College Professors, Psychologists, entertainers, musicians, authors and leaders have never weighed in on such a profound question, in aggregate, before - or since. Within their varied insights, despite their uniqueness as individuals and the very different lives they led, the reader will note a consistent thread running through their viewpoints, revealing a commonality among human beings who not only seek meaning in life, but who actually achieve it.

The reader should not expect a manual of Pollyanna platitudes, for *On The Meaning Of Life* contains no insights that are tethered to the clouds of airy whim, but rather are grounded in Durant's "real world" philosophy and his own special quality as a thinker. It is compassionate yet tough-minded, an optimistic and courageous book, which reveals to the reader examples of how their fellow human beings have stepped out of the confines of fear and worry and embraced more fully a life of authenticity, harmony and total confidence. It is a book that should be in the hands of every college graduate as he prepares to set sail upon the often stormy seas of life, and a book that should also find permanent residence in the personal libraries of family and friends, for it sheds light on an important issue and offers a renewal of hope, culminating in a positive and life-affirming answer to that great philosophical question "what is the meaning of life?"

Perhaps, as Durant feared, a mere book - even when placed in the hands of the oppressed and downtrodden - will do little to diminish their rate of suicide and enlighten their lives. But, perhaps again, it is worth the attempt.

-- John Little

---

1. Data provided by a study from the World Health Organization, reported on www.befrienders.or/info/statistics.htm).
2. Will and Ariel Durant, *Will & Ariel Durant: A Dual Autobiography*. Simon and Schuster, New York, © 1977 Will Durant. Page 168.

PART ONE:
AN APPEAL
FOR MEANING

CHAPTER ONE
A LETTER

On July 15, 1931 I sent the following letter, with variations, from my home in New York to certain famous contemporaries here and abroad for whose intelligence I had high regard:

Dear _____,

Will you interrupt your work for a moment and play the game of philosophy with me? I am attempting to face a question which our generation, perhaps more than any, seems always ready to ask and never able to answer --What is the meaning or worth of human life? Heretofore this question has been dealt with chiefly by theorists, from Ikhnaton and Lao-tzu to Bergson and Spengler. The result has been a kind of intellectual suicide: thought, by its very development, seems to have destroyed the value and significance of life. The growth and spread of knowledge, for which so many idealists and reformers prayed, has resulted in a disillusionment which has almost broken the spirit of our race.

Astronomers have told us that human affairs constitute but a moment in the trajectory of a star; geologists have told us that civilization is but a precarious interlude between ice ages; biologists have told us that all life is war, a struggle for existence among individuals, groups, nations, alliances, and species; historians have told us that "progress" is a delusion, whose glory ends in inevitable decay; psychologists have told us that the will and the self are the helpless instruments of heredity and environment, and that the once incorruptible soul is but a transient incandescence of the brain.

The Industrial Revolution has destroyed the home, and the discovery of contraceptives is destroying the family, the old, morality, and perhaps (through the sterility of the intelligent) the race. Love is analyzed into a physical congestion, and marriage becomes a temporary physiological convenience slightly superior to promiscuity. Democracy has degenerated into such corruption as only Milo's Rome knew; and our youthful dreams of a socialist Utopia disappear as we see, day after day, the inexhaustible acquisitiveness of men. Every invention strengthens the strong and weakens the weak; every new mechanism displaces men, and multiplies the horrors of war.

God, who was once the consolation of our brief life, and our refuge in bereavement and suffering, has apparently vanished from the scene; no telescope, no microscope discovers him. Life has become, in that total perspective which is philosophy, a fitful pullulation of human insects on the earth, a planetary eczema that may soon be cured; nothing is certain in it except defeat and death -- a sleep from which, it seems, there is no awakening.

We are driven to conclude that the greatest mistake in human history was the discovery of "truth." It has not made us free, except from delusions that comforted us and restraints that preserved us. It has not made us happy, for truth is not beautiful, and did not deserve to be so passionately chased. As we look on it now we wonder why we hurried so to find it. For it has taken from us every reason for existence except the moment's pleasure and tomorrow's trivial hope.

This is the pass to which science and philosophy have brought us. I, who have loved philosophy for many years, now turn back to life itself, and ask you, as one who has lived as well as thought, to help me understand. Perhaps the verdict of those who have lived is different from that of those who have merely thought. Spare me a moment to tell me what meaning life has for you, what keeps you going, what help -- if any -- religion gives you, what are the sources of your inspiration and your energy, what is the goal or motiveforce of your toil, where you find your consolations and your happiness, where, in the last resort, your treasure lies.

Write briefly if you must; write at length and at leisure if you possibly can; for every word from you will be precious to me.

Sincerely yours,
Will Durant

I would not have this letter taken as expressing very accurately my own conclusions on the meaning of our existence; I cannot find it in my nature to be so despondent. But I wished to confront at the outset the bitterest possibilities, to load the dice against my own desires, and to put the problem in such a way as to guard against the superficial optimism with which men are wont to turn aside the profounder issues of life.

And since no one deserves to believe unless he has served an apprenticeship of doubt, I propose to state at some length the case against the worth and significance of human affairs. Later we shall consider the replies which have come to this letter from various nations and continents; and in the final chapter I propose to answer the question for myself with whatever sincerity a half-century of life has left me in the face of the greatest of all temptations to lie.

CHAPTER TWO
THE PROBLEM AND RELIGION

The natural condition of humanity, and even of philosophers, is hope. Great religions arise and flourish out of the need men feel to believe in their worth and destiny; and great civilizations have normally rested upon these inspiriting religions.

Where such a faith, after supporting men for centuries, begins to weaken, life narrows down from a spiritual drama to a biological episode; it sacrifices the dignity conferred by a destiny endless in time, and shrinks to a strange interlude between a ridiculous birth and an annihilating death. Reduced to a microscopic triviality by the perspective of science, the informed individual loses belief in himself and his race, and enterprises of great pith and moment, which once aroused his effort and admiration, awaken in him only skepticism and scorn. Faith and hope disappear; doubt and despair are the order of the day.

This is the essential diagnosis of our time. It is not merely great wars that have plunged us into pessimism, much less the economic depression of these recent years; we have to do here with something far deeper than a temporary diminution of our wealth, or even the death of millions of men; it is not our homes and our treasuries that are empty, it is our "hearts." It seems impossible any longer to believe in the permanent greatness of man, or to give life a meaning that cannot be annulled by death. We move into an age of spiritual exhaustion and despondency like that which hungered for the birth of Christ.

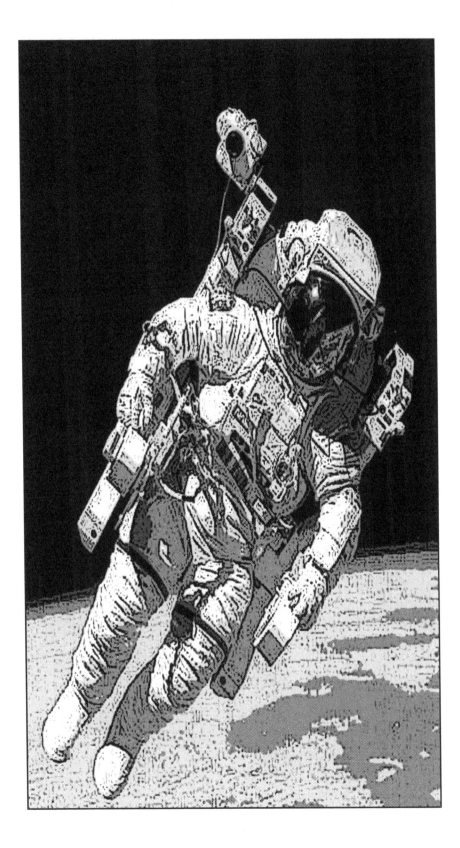

CHAPTER THREE
THE PROBLEM AND SCIENCE

When the eighteenth century laid the foundations of the nineteenth, it staked everything upon one idea -- the replacement of theology with science. Given science, and there would soon be wealth, which would make men happy; given science, and there would soon be truth, which would make men free. Universal education would spread the findings of science, liberate men from superstition, and make them fit for democracy; a century of such universal schooling, Jeremy Bentham predicted, would solve all major problems, and bring Utopia. "There is no limit to the progress of mankind," said Condorcet, "except the duration of the globe upon which it is placed." "The young are fortunate," said Voltaire, "for they will see great things."

They did. They saw the Revolution and the Terror. Waterloo and '48, Balaklava and Gettysburg, Sedan and Mukden, Armageddon and Lenin. They saw the growth and triumph of the sciences: of biology with Darwin, of physics with Faraday, of chemistry with Dalton, of astronomy with Laplace, of medicine with Pasteur, of mathematics with Einstein. All the hopes of the Enlightenment were realized: science was free, and was remaking the world. But while the technicians were using science to transform the earth, philosophers were using it to transform the universe. Slowly, as one science after another reported its findings, a picture was unfolded of universal struggle and death; and decade by decade the optimism of the nineteenth century yielded to the pessimism of today.

The astronomers reported that the earth, which had been the footstool of God and the home of the atoning Christ, was a minor planet circling about a minor sun; that it had had its birth in a violent disruption, and would end in collision and conflagration, leaving not a shadow of man's work to tell his tale. The geologists reported that life was tolerated transiently upon the earth at the pleasure of ice and heat, at the mercy of falling lava and failing rain; that oceans and mountains were engaged in a perpetual warfare of encroachment and corrosion, and alternating victory; that great continents had been destroyed by earthquakes and would be again. The paleontologists reported that a million species of animals had lived on the earth for a paltry eon or two and had disappeared without leaving anything more than a few bones and imprints in the rocks. The biologists reported that all life lives at the expense of other life, that big things eat little things and are eaten in turn; that strong organisms use and abuse weak organisms in a hundred thousand ways forever; that the ability to kill is the ultimate test of survival; that reproduction is suicide, and that love is the prelude to replacement and death.

Here, as example and symbol of all life, is my dog "Wolf," who owes her existence to the olfactory attractiveness of her police-dog mother to her collie sire. She eats greedily and drinks abstemiously (she is a teetotaler, and despite the pressure of current fashions refuses all alcoholic beverages); she chases whatever we throw, takes the coziest seats in the house, receives our affection as a matter of course, falls into a rut, and lures to our porch half a hundred lovers. All night long our neighbor's Airedale waits at our door, and moans like a Troubadour. What but bad poetry is the difference between this and love?

Later "Lady Wolf," after much commotion, suffering, and mute inquiries as to the sense and meaning of it all, litters the house with pups. She suckles them patiently, protects them growlingly against all danger, and nearly dies of their simultaneous voracity. At times she laps up milk from a bowl while her babies tug at her breasts, and then the apparently aimless circularity and repetitiousness of life leaps to the eye. One by one the pups are given away; Wolf looks for them for a day and then forgets them. The final pup exploits and maltreats her, stealing her food and snapping at her legs; she permits it all graciously, like any Madonna with her babe. When this last survivor goes in his turn, Wolf gives no sign of bereavement; she falls back into her maiden routine, and lives happily until the love-fever agitates her -- and the village -- again. Then she mates, breeds, and the cycle of life comes full turn once more.

Is not this also the essence of human life? Take away the

frills, and what greater significance than Wolf's has our own merry-go-round of births and deaths? Hidden away in the small type of our daily press, under the captions of "Births," "Marriages" and "Deaths," is the essential history of mankind -- everything else is ornament. Looked at in this canine perspective the sublime tale of Heloise and Abelard, or the lyric of Wimpole Street, are but incidents in Nature's fanatical resolution to carry on. All this hunting of a man after a maid, all this anatomical display, this revealing concealment, these luring perfumes, these graceful movements, this stealthy scrutiny, this gynecological wit, these romances and dramas and films, all this money-making, tailoring, clothes-brushing, preening, dancing, singing, tail-spreading, prattling, itching -- all are part of the ritual of reproduction. The ceremony becomes more complex, but the end is as before: unto them a little child is born.

Once the child had an immortal soul; now it has glands. To the physicist it is only a bundle of molecules, or atoms, or electrons, or protons; to the physiologist it is an unstable conjunction of muscles, bones and nerves; to the physician it is a red mass of illnesses and pains; to the psychologist it is a helpless mouthpiece of heredity and environment, a rabble of conditioned reflexes marshaled by hunger and love. Almost every idea this strange organism will have will be a delusion; almost every perception will be a prejudice. It will rear fine theories of free will and immortal life, and "from hour to hour" it will "rot and rot"; it will construct great systems of philosophy, in which the drop of water will explain the sea. The thought will seldom occur to this "forked radish" called man that it is just one species among a billion, a passing experiment of Nature, who, as Turgeniev said, entertains no preferences as between men and fleas.

Only science gives us at last the gift which Robert Burns unwisely begged of the gods -- to see ourselves as others see us, even as other species see us. In the end we perceive that to the dog we are but irrational prattlers, making much noise with the tongue; and that to the mosquito we are merely meals. Some of us reach the last stage of objectivity, and surrender our final prejudice, the judgment of beauty; we admit that something may be said for the Zulu's idolatry of adipose mates, and that a Martian might conceivably admire, next to the beauty of collies and mares, the loveliness of woman. Slowly we cease to be the center and summit of the universe; our species -- in the scientific eye -- are trivial fragments, flying off at a tangent towards destruction.

CHAPTER FOUR
THE PROBLEM AND HISTORY

The nineteenth century was the age of history as well as of science; the hunger for facts turned with a concerted fury upon the past, dismembered and dissected it, and discovered the rise and fall of nations. The resultant picture is a panorama of development and decay; history, as Bacon said, is the planks of a shipwreck, and nothing seems certain in it except decadence, degeneration, and death.

A thousand varieties of man -- Piltdown, Neanderthal, Chellean, Acheulean, Mousterian, Aurignacian, Cro-magnon, Rhodesian, Pekin man -- lived for thousands of years, fought, thought, invented, painted, carved, made children, and left no more to posterity than a few flints and scratches, forgotten for millennia and found only by the picks and spades of our inquisitive day.

A thousand civilizations have disappeared under the ocean or the earth, leaving, like Atlantis, merely a legend behind; Turkestan, Mohenjo-Daru, Ur of the Chaldees, Samarkand of Tamerlane, Angkor of the Khmers, Yucatan of the Mayas, and the Incas' Peru -- these are the mausolea of cultures almost completely lost. They are among the few which we have unearthed; calculate, then, the number of dead civilizations of which history preserves no vestige at all. And of the pitiful minority that have clung to some place in human memory -- like Babylon and Egypt, Persia and Crete, Greece and Rome -- consider their grandeur and decadence, and see how uncertain a thing history is, how its greatest names are writ in water, and how even Shakespeare may become to his countrymen, within a century of his death, a half-forgotten barbarian given to melodramatic fustian and bad puns.

All things, said Aristotle, have been discovered and forgotten many times over. Progress, he assures us, is a delusion; human affairs are like the sea, which on its surface is disturbed into a thousand motions, and seems to be headed somewhere, while at its bottom it is comparatively changeless and still. What we call progress is, perhaps, mere superficial change: a succession of fashions in dress, transportation, government, psychology, religion; Christian Science, behaviorism, democracy, automobiles, and pants are not progress, they are change; they are new ways of doing old things, new errors in the vain attempt to understand eternal mysteries. Underneath these varying phenomena the essence remains the same; the man who uses the steam shovel and the electric drill, the tractor and the tank, the adding-machine and the machinegun, the airplane and the bomb, is the same sort of man as those who used wooden ploughs, flint knives, log wheels, bows and arrows, knot writing, and poisoned spear-heads; the tool differs, the end is the same; the scale is vaster, the purposes as crude and selfish, as stupid and contradictory, as murderous and suicidal, as in prehistoric or ancient days; everything has progressed except man.

All history, then, all the proud record of human accumulations and discoveries, seems at times to be a futile circle, a weary tragedy in which Sisyphus man repeatedly pushes invention and labor up the high hill of civilization and culture, only to have the precarious structure again and again topple back into barbarism -- into coolies, ryots, fellaheen, moujiks and serfs -- through the exhaustion of the soil, or the migrations of trade, or the vandalism of invaders, or the educated sterility of the race. So much remains of Condorcet's "indefinite perfectibility of mankind." Indefinite indeed.

CHAPTER FIVE
THE PROBLEM AND UTOPIAS

All the dogma that in the last one hundred years gave to earthly life something of the significance which the hope of heaven brought to medieval man, seems to have lost countenance in this skeptical century. "Progress," "universal education," "popular sovereignty" -- who is now so poor in doubt as to do them reverence?

Our schools are like our inventions -- they offer us new ideas, new means of doing old things; they elevate us from petty larceny to bank wreckages and Teapot Domes. They stake all on intellect, only to find that character wins in the end. We taught people how to read, and they enrich the "tabloids" and motion pictures; we invented the radio, and they pour out, a hundred times more abundantly than before, the music of savages and the prejudices of mobs. We gave them, through technology and engineering, unprecedented wealth -- miraculous automobiles, luxurious travel, and spacious homes; only to find that peace departs as riches come, that automobiles over-ride morality and connive at crime, that quarrels grow bitterer as the spoils increase, and that the largest houses are the bloodiest battlegrounds of the ancient war between woman and man.

We discovered birth control, and now it sterilizes the intelligent, multiplies the ignorant, debases love with promiscuity, frustrates the educator, empowers the demagogue, and deteriorates the race. We enfranchised all men, and find them supporting and preserving, in nearly every city, a nefarious "machine" that blocks the road between ability and office; we enfranchised all women, and discovered that nothing is changed except clerical expense. We dreamed of socialism, and found our own souls too greedy to make it possible; in our hearts we too are capitalists, and have no serious objection to becoming rich.

We dreamed of emancipation through organized labor, and found great unions working hand in hand with corrupt machines and murderous gangs; these are the instruments with which we poor intellectuals planned to build Utopia. We turned at last to Russia, and found it conquering poverty at the cost of that freedom of body and mind, of work and thought, which has been the soul of liberalism and radicalism from Godwin to Darrow, from Emerson to Kropotkin, from Rabelais to Anatole France.

And over all the drama hovers, like a many-armed Shiva, the merry god of war. The grandeur of Egypt is the child of brutal conquest and despotism; the glory of Greece is rooted in the mire of slavery; the majesty of Rome is in its triremes and its legions; the civilization of Europe rises and falls with its guns. History, like Napoleon's God, is on the side of Big Bertha; it laughs at artists and philosophers, destroys their work in a moment of patriotism, and gives its honors, its statues and its pages to Mars. Egypt builds and Persia destroys it; Persia builds and Greece destroys it; Greece builds and Rome destroys it; Islam builds and Spain destroys it; Spain builds and England destroys it; Europe builds and Europe destroys it. Men kill one another at first with sticks and stones, then with arrows and lances, then with phalanxes and cohorts, then with cannon and musketry, then with dreadnoughts and submarines, then with tanks and planes; the scale and grandeur of construction and progress are equaled by the scale and terror of destruction and war. One by one the nations rear their heads in pride, and one by one war decapitates them. "Look on my works, ye mighty, and despair," reads the proud inscription on the ruined and desolate statue of Ozymandias, builder of buildings and "King of Kings"; but the traveler reports, simply:

Nothing beside remains. Round the decay
Of that colossal wreck, boundless and bare
The lone and level sands stretch far away.

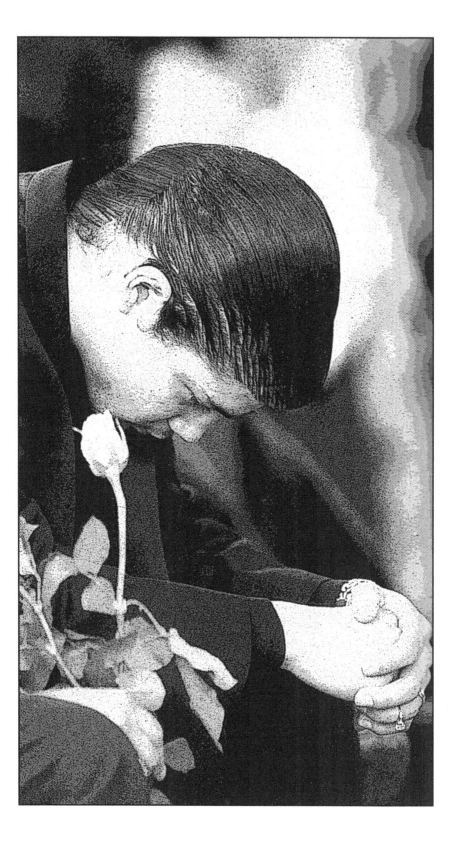

CHAPTER SIX
THE SUICIDE OF THE INTELLECT

In the face of this impartial destructiveness of history --
this neutrality of nature between good and evil, life and death
-- the soul of man, in the past, has strengthened itself with
faith in a juster world to come. There all these wrongs would
be righted, and the poor man in heaven would have the
pleasure of letting a drop of water fall upon the rich man's
tongue in hell.

There was something ferocious in the old faiths; the gentle gospels of Buddha and Christ were blackened by time into
holy orgies of revenge; every paradise had its inferno, to
which good people fervently consigned those who had succeeded too well in life, or had adopted the wrong myth. In
those "happy days" men agreed that life was evil: Gautama
called the extinction of individual consciousness the greatest
good, and the Church described life as a vale of tears. Men
could afford to be pessimists about the earth, because they
were optimists about the sky; behind those clouds they saw
the isles of the blest, the abode of everlasting bliss.

As I write a song comes up from the street below. A black-
garbed lass, accompanied by a tremulous brass band, is
singing *The Rock of Ages*. Silently I join in the refrain and all
the idealized memories of my pious youth surge up within
me. I slip down and pass among the impromptu congregation
that has gathered about the singers. The uniformed men in
the official band do not impress me; without exception they
are hard-looking, practical fellows. Long since, I fear, religion
has become a business with them. The uniformed women,
whose shrill voices carry the burden of the song, are pale and
thin, empty in body and soul; everything spiritual dies when it
is sold, or made a motley to the view.

But in the crowd itself the faces are not hard. These men
seem for the most part destitute -- jobless and penniless; the
exploitation and poverty that are a part of life have fallen
heavily upon them; they are one moment in the eternal
wastage of selection. Yet they are not bitter; they listen
patiently to the harangue of the preacher calling them violent-

ly to the gentle Christ. Despite his invectives and denunciations some of them seem comforted; for a while they catch a glimpse of another world than their daily round of unemployment and fruitless search, of burning hunger and weary feet. In a dark doorway an old woman listens hopefully, sheds a tear, and mumbles a prayer. But for the most part the men smile incredulously; their poverty does not seem to them to declare the glory of God. When the song is renewed not one of them joins in it; one by one they walk quietly away. Even into these simple souls the skepticism of our time has entered. How shall I, fortunate and comfortable, ever fathom the despair of these men, shorn not only of the goods of life but of a consoling faith as well?

For today science, which, because of its marvelous creations, they have learned to trust as once they trusted the priest, has told them that the sky which of old promised them happiness, is mere blue nothing, cold and empty space, and that those clouds among which the angels frolicked are only the steaming perspiration of the earth.

Science does not offer consolation, it offers death. Everything, from the unwinding universe of the astronomers to the college girl irradiating life with beauty and laughter, must pass away: this handsome youth, erect and vigorous, fresh from athletic victories, will be laid low tomorrow by some modest, ingratiating germ; this noble pianist, who has dignified his time with perfection, and has taught a million souls to forget themselves in beauty, is already in the clutch of death, and will, within a decade, be rotting in the tomb.

The greatest question of our time is not communism vs. individualism, not Europe vs. America, not even the East vs. the West; it is whether men can bear to live without God. Religion was profounder than philosophy, and refused to root human happiness in the earth; it based man's hopes where knowledge could never reach them -- beyond the grave.

Perhaps Asia was profounder than Europe, and medievalism profounder than modernity; for they kept at arm's length this science that seems to kill whatever it touches, reducing soul to brain, life to matter, personality to chemistry, and will to fate. Perhaps some confident and stoic race, still strong in religious enthusiasm, will engulf and absorb these disillusioned peoples of the West, so scientifically in love with death.

This, then, is the final triumph of thought -- that it disintegrates all societies, and at last destroys the thinker himself. Perhaps the invention of thought was one of the cardinal errors of mankind. For first, thought undermined morality by shearing it of its supernatural sanctions and sanctity, and revealing it as a social utility designed to save policemen; and a morality without God is as weak as a traffic law when the policeman is on foot. Second, thought undermined society by separating sex from parentage, removing the penalty from promiscuity, and liberating the individual from the race; now only the ignorant transmit their kind. Finally it undermined the thinker by revealing to him, in astronomy and geology, biology and history, a panorama in which he saw himself as an insignificant fragment in space and a flickering moment in time; it took from him his belief in his own will and future, left his fate nude of nobility and grandeur, and weakened him into despondency and surrender.

And here, in the *macabre finale*, philosophy joins hands with science in the work of destruction. That total perspective which it preached so proudly and so eagerly pursued is apparently the most dangerous -- though the rarest -- foe of resolution and joy; for what meaning or dignity can the individual have in a world so vast, among species without number, and in time without end? He that increaseth knowledge increaseth sorrow, and in much wisdom is much vanity.

This is the challenge which confronts our age, and dwarfs all other problems of philosophy and religion, economics and statesmanship; beside it the apparent ruin of our economic system becomes a transitory trifle unworthy of serious concern. If the reader has been disturbed by these pages, it is good; let him now find in his own mental resources some basis for his faith; let him honestly formulate his own reply to this philosophy of despair. For those of us who wish to live consciously, to know the worst and praise the best, must meet all these doubts if we are to maintain any longer our pretense to the life of reason.

PART TWO:
THOUGHTS ON OUR
PRESENT DISCONTENT

CHAPTER SEVEN
THE MEN OF LETTERS RESPOND

The letter printed at the beginning of this book was sent, in the summer of 1931, to a hundred or more of the then brighter luminaries in contemporary life and thought. In each case the letter was accompanied by a request for permission to publish the reply. A considerable number of the addressed begged to be excused from answering, lest they incriminate themselves; public officials in particular were reluctant to speak frankly on so delicate a question, since their tenure of office depended (in some slight measure) on the goodwill of the uninformed. I can readily forgive them; I confess that my letter involved too intimate a scrutiny of private opinions for public lives; and I know the heavy price which must be paid in amiable hypocrisy for the privilege of holding office in a democratic state.

Theodore Dreiser

Under the circumstances I was surprised by the abundance and candor of the replies. Our greatest novelist, Theodore Dreiser, immersed in the battles of the unemployed, wrote briefly, under date of June 23rd, 1931:

> Your letter of June 15th seems to me the best answer that can be made to your question: "What is the meaning or worth of human life?" If I had the time to undertake such a task as you suggest, my answer would really be some such diatribe as this letter of yours.

H.L. Mencken

From our leading critic, H. L. Mencken, the man who above all others has influenced contemporary American literature and thought, came this frank reply:

> You ask me, in brief, what satisfaction I get out of life, and why I go on working. I go on working for the same reason that a hen goes on laying eggs. There is in every living creature

an obscure but powerful impulse to active functioning. Life demands to be lived. Inaction, save as a measure of recuperation between bursts of activity, is painful and dangerous to the healthy organism -- in fact, it is almost impossible. Only the dying can be really idle.

The precise form of an individual's activity is determined, of course, by the equipment with which he came into the world. In other words, it is determined by his heredity. I do not lay eggs, as a hen does, because I was born without any equipment for it. For the same reason I do not get myself elected to Congress, or play the violoncello, or teach metaphysics in a college, or work in a steel mill. What I do is simply what lies easiest to my hand. It happens that I was born with an intense and insatiable interest in ideas, and, thus, like to play with them. It happens also that I was born with rather more than the average facility for putting them into words. In consequence, I am a writer and editor; which is to say, a dealer in them and concoctor of them.

There is very little conscious volition in all this. What I do was ordained by the inscrutable fates, not chosen by me. In my boyhood, yielding to a powerful but still subordinate interest in exact facts, I wanted to be a chemist, and at the same time my poor father tried to make me a businessman. At other times, like any other relatively poor man, I have longed to make a lot of money by some easy swindle. But I became a writer all the same, and shall remain one until the end of the chapter, just as a cow goes on giving milk all her life, even though what appears to be her self-interest urges her to give gin.

I am far luckier than most men, for I have been able since boyhood to make a good living doing precisely what I have wanted to do -- what I would have done for nothing, and very gladly, if there had been no reward for it. Not many men, I believe, are so fortunate. Millions of them have to make their livings at tasks which really do not interest them. As for me, I have had an extraordinarily pleasant life, despite the fact that I have had the usual share of woes. For in the midst of those woes I still enjoyed the immense satisfaction which goes with free activity. I have done, in the main, exactly what I wanted to do. Its possible effects upon other people have interested me very little. I have not written and published to please other people, but to satisfy myself, just as a cow gives milk, not to profit the dairyman, but to satisfy herself. I like to think that most of my ideas have been sound ones, but I really don't care. The world may take them or leave them. I have had my fun hatching them.

Next to agreeable work as a means of attaining happiness I put what Huxley called the "domestic affections" -- the day-to-day intercourse with family and friends. My home has seen bitter sorrow, but it has never seen any serious disputes, and it has never seen poverty. I was completely happy with my mother and sister, and I am completely happy with my wife.

Most of the men I commonly associate with are friends of very old standing. I have known some of them for more than thirty years. I seldom see anyone, intimately, whom I have known for less than ten years. These friends delight me. I turn to them when work is done with unfailing eagerness. We have the same general tastes, and see the world much alike. Most of them are interested in music, as I am. It has given me more pleasure in this life than any other external thing. I love it more every year.

As for religion, I am quite devoid of it. Never in my adult life have I experienced anything that could be plausibly called a religious impulse. My father and grandfather were agnostics before me, and though I was sent to Sunday school as a boy and exposed to the Christian theology I was never taught to believe it. My father thought that I should learn what it was, but it apparently never occurred to him that I would accept it. He was a good psychologist. What I got in Sunday school -- beside a wide acquaintance with Christian hymnology -- was simply a firm conviction that the Christian faith was full of palpable absurdities, and the Christian God preposterous. Since that time I have read a great deal in theology -- perhaps much more than the average clergyman -- but I have never discovered any reason to change my mind.

The act of worship, as carried on by Christians, seems to me to be debasing rather than ennobling. It involves groveling before a Being who, if He really exists, deserves to be denounced instead of respected. I see little evidence in this world of the so-called goodness of God. On the contrary, it seems to me that, on the strength of His daily acts, He must be set down a most stupid, cruel and villainous fellow. I can say this with a clear conscience, for He has treated me very well -- in fact, with vast politeness. But I can't help thinking of his barbaric torture of most of the rest of humanity. I simply can't imagine revering the God of war and politics, theology and cancer.

I do not believe in immortality, and have no desire for it. The belief in it issues from the puerile egos of inferior men. In its Christian form it is little more than a device for getting revenge upon those who are having a better time on this earth. What the meaning of human life may be I don't know: I incline to suspect that it has none. All I know about it is that, to me at least, it is very amusing while it lasts. Even its troubles, indeed, can be amusing. Moreover, they tend to foster the human qualities that I admire most -- courage and its analogues. The noblest man, I think, is that one who fights God, and triumphs over Him. I have had little of this to do. When I die I shall be content to vanish into nothingness. No show, however good, could conceivably be good forever.

This is a delightful piece, which I print here with the uneasy conscience of a man stealing a gem; I trust Mr. Mencken will do me the honor some day of appropriating something of mine, if he can find in me anything so honest and modest as this auto-analysis of Mencken in terms of cows and hens. The man here revealed is a being more diverse and sensitive than the editor of the *American Mercury*; he is not afraid to "love" music and his home, and braves all the conventions of our literary world by getting along with his wife -- though he was clever enough to marry at an age when monogamy is bearable.

Perhaps because he fears and distrusts this secret sensitivity and tenderness in his nature he clings to a hard, "tough-minded" philosophy of mechanism and determinism and will confess no sympathy with the eternal hunger of mankind for supernatural consolations. It is doubtful if we shall find in all our batch of answers a reply so straightforward as this.

Mr. Mencken is commonly rated and berated as a pessimist, but it is evidently possible for a man to be a pessimist about the world and yet a tolerably cheerful fellow in his life.

Sinclair Lewis

So with our most famous novelist, Sinclair Lewis: he has no very ingratiating opinion of us poor hypocrites, and might be judged from his books to be a man full of irony and gall; but his simple letter indicates how unnecessary it is to conclude from mechanism and atheism to sorrow and despair:

> It is, I think, an error to believe that there is any need of religion to make life seem worth living, or to give consolation in sorrow, except in the case of people who have been reared to religion so that should they lose it in their adult years, they would miss it, their whole thinking having been conditioned by it.

I know several young people who have been reared entirely without thought of churches, of formal theology, or any other aspect of religion, who have learned ethics not as a divine commandment but as a matter of social convenience. They seem to me quite as happy, quite as filled with purpose and with eagerness about life as any one trained to pass all his troubles on to the Lord, or the Lord's local agent, the pastor. Their satisfaction comes from functioning healthily, from physical and mental exercise, whether it be playing tennis or tackling an astronomical problem.

Nor do I believe that most of them will even in old age feel any need of religious consolation, because I know also a few old people who have been thus reared all their lives and who are perfectly serene just to be living. A seventy-four-year-old agnostic like Clarence Darrow is not less but more cheerful and excited about life's adventure -- yes, and 'spiritual minded' -- than an aged bishop whose bright hopes of Heaven are often overbalanced by his fears of Hell.

If I go to a play I do not enjoy it less because I do not believe that it is divinely created and divinely conducted, that it will last forever instead of stopping at eleven, that many details of it will remain in my memory after a few months, or that it will have any particular moral effect upon me. And I enjoy life as I enjoy that play.

If you wish to quote any of this, you may.

Sincerely yours,

Sinclair Lewis

All three of these replies take mechanism or materialism for granted; this is the secret base upon which the most characteristic achievements of that era's literature were built. The philosophy of one age is the literature of the next; the novels and dramas of that era -- the work of Mann and Schnitzler, Gorki and Wells, Dreiser and Lewis, Toller and O'Neill -- are echoes of Darwin and Spencer, Nietzsche and Karl Marx. Shaw moved up to Bergson, and O'Neill added Freud to Schopenhauer to become the American Sophocles. Literature had not yet discovered that the science of 1932 seriously questioned the philosophy of 1859.

John Erskine

I speak inaccurately; not all of our leading writers from

that era came under the banner of a mechanist creed. John Erskine had some doubts which he expressed with characteristic urbanity and tolerance:

Dear Mr. Durant,

It seems to be that the human race has been given to two bad mistakes in its thinking. One is to forget that our spiritual life is just as natural as our physical. Whether or not the philosophers care to admit that we have a soul, it seems obvious that we are equipped with something or other which generates dreams and ideals, and which sets up values. My own disposition is to accept in its entirety this human nature which we are born to, without splitting too many hairs as to whether that nature is dual or single. It is natural to me, and I assume for others as well, to imagine ultimate ends and to worship those ends as our God. It does not disturb me that man's conception of God varies greatly at different times and in different places. Apparently that variation is a condition of our nature in this world.

To think of life in these terms is, I suppose, to define religion as an art, as something which man will surely put forth out of himself whether it emerges as Mohammedanism, or Catholicism or as the present Communism of Russia. If some of us are offended by the description of religion as an art, it is probably because they do not attach the importance which I do to art. I should like to use the word to cover all the ideal-making and ideal-expressing functions of our nature....

If it is a mistake not to recognize that our spiritual life is as natural as our physical, it is another and probably a more common error to confuse our spiritual ideals with the actual facts of existence. If we were willing to follow our ideals as ideals -- as ends which we hope to achieve -- we could then perhaps be gentle with our fellow man who has other purposes. But an intense faith, if one can judge from history, often makes us stupidly literal....

To say that life is an art would imply to some people that the description of human nature here given makes too little of the moral sense. I believe that the sanctions of morality are implicit in the human instinct to make of life a work of art. Though we sometimes speak of a primrose path, we all know that a bad life is just as difficult, just as full of obstacles and hardships, as a good one. We are told that the way is strait which leads to salvation; we are also told that the way of the transgressor is hard. The only choice is in the kind of life one would care to spend one's efforts on. I believe the divine element in man is whatever it is which makes us wish to lead a life worth remembering, harmless to others, helpful to them, and increasing our own store of wisdom and peace.

Faithfully yours,

John Erskine

Charles Beard

And Charles Beard, one of the soundest minds of that generation, wrote with the uncertainty of a modest man dealing with infinites:

My Dear Will Durant,

The question you propound is important, the most important that could be asked, and therefore difficult to answer, if not impossible. Still, it must be faced, and now that my shadows fall aslant to the East I am asking it with increasing anxiety. Long ago the poet Milton, I think it was, said that truth comes to us first in "hideous mien," meaning that it disturbs our old delusions and assurances. Yet in time we become familiar with it and assimilate it to life as it must be lived.

So we go on working even when some of our cherished ideals seem crushed to earth never to rise again. Why? We do not know. We can only guess. One answer is that we are driven by the biological force within us, by the necessity of earning a living, and discharging the obligations which we have gathered on the way. But that is not enough. Thousands go on working after they have secured an abundance of the good things men prize. Others keep on working, as did William Lloyd Garrison, amid the gathering gloom of apparent defeat.

When we analyze ourselves we find conflicting motives. We have moments of shivering selfishness, when we think only of our personal gain. And we have moments of exaltation when we feel the thrill of the prodigious and hear the call to high action. That seems to be true of all men and women, high and low, and the outcome in each case is a matter of proportion.

For myself I may say that as I look over the grand drama of history, I find (or seem to find) amid the apparent chaos and tragedy, evidence of law and plan and immense achievement of the human spirit in spite of disasters. I am convinced that the world is not a mere bog in which men and women trample themselves in the mire and die. Something magnificent is taking place here amid the cruelties and tragedies, and the supreme challenge to intelligence is that of making the noblest and best in our curious heritage prevail. If there was no grand design in the beginning of the universe, fragments of one are evident and mankind can complete the picture. A knowledge of the good life is our certain philosophic heritage, and technology has given us a power over nature which enables us to provide the conditions of the good life for all the earth's multitudes. That seems to me to be the most engaging possibility of the drama, and faith in its potentialities keeps me working at it even in the worst hours of disillusionment. The good life -- an end in itself to be loved and enjoyed; and intelligent labor directed to the task of making the good life prevail. There is the little philosophy, the circle of thought, within which I keep my little mill turning.

This is the appearance of things as I see them, and even profound philosophers can merely say what they find here.

Sincerely Yours,

Charles A. Beard

John Cowper Powys

The clearest expression of the idealism that lurks in the literary soul behind the modern mask came from John Cowper Powys, who was, I should say, the profoundest and subtlest and noblest genius whom I have ever met:

Dear Mr. Durant,

The collapse of organized supernaturalism and the absence, from the organized polities of the world, of any essential social liberty or culture, throws the individual back upon himself. For himself and in himself he can rediscover the secrets of faith, of hope, of happiness.

The most magical powers, values, sensations of these secrets of life are still to be found in Nature; and can be enjoyed by the weak quite as much as by the strong. The fresh-water-springs of a mystical personal life are entirely beyond the power of the passing fashions of thought to destroy; and they can exist under any system of political and economic organization or disorganization. Nature is friendly to the weak as well as to the strong; and truth does not lie in rational generalizations of laws and methods, but in an instinctive growth, implying a hardly-won and hardly-kept organic process of delicate adjustments between the individual consciousness and Nature.

Personal experience of the mystery of Nature and the mystery of Life brings back faith in the freedom of the will, faith in the powers of the soul, faith in the mystical interpretations of existence. No rational fashions of the passing hour have the least importance when it is a question of the individual consciousness adapting itself to Nature, finding its own work, its own beauty, its own truth, its own righteousness, its own happiness, and treating everything else with ironic diffidence and indulgence.

In opposition to the scientific attitude to Nature, the individual self must resort to the personal attitude and practice what Spengler, interpreting Goethe, calls the *physiognomic vision*, a vision, namely, that carries a fresh and child-like admiration of natural phenomena, as well as a wary and peasant-like suspicion of all generalizations and explanations.

To restore to one's individual life a certain secret liberty of thought and feeling, that shall be at once reverential and skeptical; to free the fresh-water-springs of one's happiness from dependence upon outward conditions while one twists outward conditions as craftily as possible to the demands of the flesh and the spirit; to compromise in un-essentials while one clings to essentials with the fluid obstinacy of water seeking its level; to retain an open mind with regard to the *magical*, while one exploits in their place and under their limitations, the *rational* interpretations of Nature and Life; to free oneself from the morbidities of sympathy as well as from the cruelties of selfishness; to treat the whole spectacle ultimately as a dream within a dream, from which it still remains possible that death may awaken us; to have no convictions except the conviction that all cruelty is evil and that all lives are holy and sacred; thus it seems to me one may reduce the astronomical universe to its due place of secondary importance compared with the concentration upon the mystery of consciousness wherein lies that "earnestness that alone makes life eternity."

John Cowper Powys

The poet -- and Powys is a poet by the compulsion of his blood -- cannot be expected to accept the harsh decrees of a materialistic philosophy; he is normally tender-minded; and even when he flaunts his atheism, like a college athlete's letter, to the world, he is apt to go on singing hymns even to the gods whom he denies, as Swinburne did, or Shelley, or Keats. For poetry dies at the touch of the mechanical, and flourishes on the theme of life and growth; it is pledged almost from the start to a spiritual interpretation of the world. Hear the vigorous rejection of mechanism by our greatest American poet:

Edwin Arlington Robinson

Dear Dr. Durant:

I have delayed my acknowledgement of your letter only for the lack of anything especially profound or valuable to say in reply to it. I told a philosopher once that all the other philosophers would have to go out of business if one of them should happen to discover the truth; and now you say, or imply, in your letter that the truth has been discovered, and that we are only the worse off, if possible, for the discovery. This is naturally a cause of some chagrin and humiliation for me, for I had heard nothing about it. It is true that we have acquired a great deal of material knowledge in recent years, but so far as knowledge of the truth itself is concerned, I cannot see that we are any nearer to it now than our less imaginative ancestors were when they cracked each others' skulls with stone hatchets, or that we know any more than they knew of what happened to the soul that escaped in the process.

It is easy, and just now rather fashionable, to say that there is no soul, but we do not know whether there is a soul or not. If a man is a materialist, or a mechanist, or whatever he likes to call himself, I can see for him no escape from belief in a futility so prolonged and complicated and diabolical and preposterous as to be worse than absurd; and as I do not know that such a tragic absurdity is not a fact, I can only know my native inability to believe that it is one. There is nothing in the thought of annihilation that frightens me; for it would be, at the worst, nothing more terrible than going to sleep at the end of a long day, whether a pleasant or a painful one, or both. But if life is only what it appears to be, no amount of improvement or enlightenment will ever compensate or atone for what it has inflicted and endured in ages past, or for what it is inflicting and enduring today. . . There is apparently not much that anyone can do about it except to follow his own light -- which may or may not be the light of an ignis fatuus in a swamp.

The cocksureness of the modern "mechanist" means nothing to me; and I doubt if it means any more to him when he pauses really to think. His position is not entirely unlike that of an intrepid explorer standing on a promontory in a fog, looking through the newest thing in the way of glasses for an ocean that he cannot see, and shouting to his mechanistic friends behind him that he has found the end of the world.

These remarks, which to some readers might seem a little severe, are more the result of observation and reflection than of personal discomfort or dissatisfaction. As lives go, my own life would be called, and properly, a rather fortunate one.

Yours Very Truly,

Edwin Arlington Robinson

Andre Maurois

But all these replies are from Americans. I pass at once to a reply from France, a contribution of the first order, and unstintedly generous. The author of *Ariel, Byron, and Disraeli* wrote as follows, but in impeccable French:

Dear Mr. Durant,

Pardon me for replying so tardily to your letter. The excuses are two: first, that I have been away from Paris, and your inquiry therefore took a long time reaching me; second, that I found the problem so interesting that I have written an entire essay in answer. I am sending it to you, and naturally I authorize you to publish a part of this should it seem desirable to you. I shall publish it myself, doubtless, in some future volume of essays.

Very Sincerely,

Andre Maurois

The essay which Monsiour Maurois composed for our little symposium is a gem worthy of Voltaire or Anatole France. He describes a successful rocket-flight of a group of Englishmen and Englishwomen to the moon. Arrived there they fail to construct, as they had planned, a rocket to return to, or communicate with, the earth, and they are compelled to make the moon their permanent home. Ten years pass. "Meanwhile all these English ladies and gentlemen continued to conduct themselves as if they were in England. The governor, Sir Charles Solomon, and Lady Solomon dressed every evening for dinner. On the King's birthday Sir Charles gave a toast to His Majesty; and all the lunar colonists murmured 'The King.' It was a moving spectacle."

Two hundred years pass, and still no word of intercourse with the earth. The seventh generation finds it difficult to believe any longer in that distant King, always invisible and always silent, of whom their credulous elders have transmitted to them a vague tradition. A group of impious students arise who flatly deny the existence of this "King of Great Britain and Ireland, Emperor of the Indies, and Protector of the Moon," in whose name all laws are promulgated and in whom all morals have had their solemn sanction. To which the Conservatives reply irritably: "Take care; if you empty the Earth of our King, and of the legendary Englishmen who have bequeathed us our traditions, you will make lunary life very difficult. For what then will be for you the meaning of this life? What will be the sources of your energy? By what secret treasure will you live?"

In the end the radicals prevail. "It is a period of melancholy and romantic despair of the young men of the moon. Experiments in sexual liberty produce a great disorder of mind and soul. Boredom follows liberty, and revolt follows boredom. People are discontent, men are troubled, and literature is excellent." A great philosopher appears who, in lyric prose, chides the disillusionment of his time:

"Why," he asks, "search for the meaning of life outside of life itself? The King of whom our legends speak -- does he exist? I do not know, and it does not matter. I know that the mountains of the moon are beautiful when the crescent of the earth illuminates them. If the King remains, as always since my birth, invisible and silent, I shall doubt his reality; but I shall not doubt life, or the beauty of the moment, or the happiness of action. Sophists teach you today that life is only a brief moment in the trajectory of a star; they tell you that nothing is certain except defeat and death. As for me, I tell you that nothing exists except victory and life. What shall we know of our death? Either the soul is immortal and we shall not die, or it perishes with the flesh and we shall not know that we are dead. Live, then, as if you were eternal, and do not believe that your life is changed merely because it seems proved that the Earth is empty. You do not live in the Earth, you live in yourself."

"Yes," Maurois tells himself, "this story would be a possible answer to the American inquirer." But, not quite satisfied with it, he casts about for another world for his thought. He sees two lines of ants crawling over a path in the park: one going from the ant-heap, the other returning to it; both engaged in some "public utility." And he imagines a philosophic ant, "with agitated antennae," stopping one of the columns with sage discourse:

"My sisters, you have believed, and I have believed with you, that the world of ants was the only important world; that the Great Ant watched over it, and that devotion to the ant-heap was a sentiment so lofty and noble as to justify all our toil and our suffering. Certainly it is hard to transport, with never a moment of rest, across these immense and perilous deserts, these bits of straw and these dead insects. It is heroic to brave the water, the landslides, birds that devour us, and these enormous forked masses which loom up in the sky in their rhythmic advance and crush hundreds of ants. This heroism, I used to believe, is easy when one devotes one's self to the greater glory of the ant-heap.

"But alas, my sisters, I have studied and reflected; and behold what I have learned: Our ant-heap, which we thought the center of the universe and the object of particular attention from the Great Ant, resembles a thousand ant-heaps, each of which is inhabited by thousands of ants, each of which thinks that his city is the navel of the world. You are astonished? But this is nothing yet. Though the ants form a race so vast that one could never number them, they are, nevertheless, only one race among thousands of races, one form among the infinitely many forms of life. You protest, dear ants? But there is more. Not only is the ant merely one form among forms; it is -- though it costs my pride much to say it -- one of the feeblest and most contemptible of forms. These forked monsters who crush us in the sand think it a humiliation to say to themselves: 'We, in the sight of God, are no more than the ants.' You threaten me? You are indignant? . . . . Ah, dear ants, you may well pardon these monsters, for they, too, are deceived by their pride even in the moment of their humility; this earth of which they think themselves masters is but a drop of mud, and the duration of their race is but an instant in eternity.

"This, my sisters, is what I have learned in observing men, the movements of the sand, and the courses of the stars.

Having seen that all is vanity, I say to you: Why work? Why transport these bits of sand, these corpses of butterflies? Why traverse these dangerous deserts in long and toiling processions ? What will be the fruit of your labor on this earth? You will raise another generation of ants which in its turn will labor, suffer, and be crushed by the large feet of men. And these ants in turn will bring up other ants, even to that time -- infinitely far and infinitely near -- when the Earth will be only a dead world. Therefore I say to you: Stop; cease from this useless slavery; be no longer dupes. Know that there is no Great Ant above us, that progress is an illusion, that your desire to toil is but the result of heredity, that nothing is certain on the Earth except the defeat and death of the ants -- a sleep from which there is no awakening."

But a young ant politely pushes the Sage Ant aside. "This is all very well, sister," he says, "but we must build our tunnel." And Maurois again concludes:

"This story too would be a possible reply to the American philosopher. Science, he says, teaches that the life of our societies is only a pullulation of human insects on the Earth, a planetary moss or mold. But does not the insect itself wish to live? Does not even the mold persevere in its being? And is it true that science destroys the faith of man in himself? What has science done, if not to give man powerful formulae for the transformation of his world? Man was a mold before science as well as after it; science has done nothing except to make this human mold master of the earth.

"The American philosopher will reply: 'What has been changed is this -- that before science came this human moss did not know itself as moss, these insects did not know that they were only insects. They believed in the high dignity of man. Devils, angels and gods, always hovering over them, dictated their actions. Hope of a future life made them forget the sorrows of earthly existence. Rites and laws, supported by a supernatural authority, saved men from anguish and doubt. But what gods lend to law today the force of their name? Osiris replaced the god of the tribe, Jupiter replaced Osiris, Jehovah replaced Jupiter. But can the name of Einstein or Eddington serve to impose limits upon human desire?'

"A light wind made the shadows of the roller blinds tremble on the white walls. It is true, I thought, that man cannot live without rules. But an instinct preserves him from such a calamity; as soon as one web of law and morals is torn from him, instinct weaves another to protect him. Sometimes it makes such a web out of the commandments of God; some-times out of the counsels of science, sometimes out of the decrees of an earthly king. What difference does it make? Suppress if we will, like our Englishmen in the moon, the real-ity of the symbol; do the laws become less wise than before? Shall we not end by accepting these laws as necessary, though changing, conventions? Shall we not confess, at last, that every proposition which goes beyond human experience is uncertain? We know only that we do not know. Is this so terrible a confession? Is it a new idea, and did Socrates never utter it?

"Twilight came. Already the inn-keeper, in suspenders, brought out his chair to the sidewalk. Lights appeared in the windows of the townsfolk, shining upon full tables. What is my secret treasure? I asked myself. This horror of a doctrine? This love of action? Behind the roofs, suddenly grown dark, a milky clearness ran across the sky. The moon rose."

Let us pause here for a while; it would not do to spoil this fine bit of philosophical imagination with any lesser note.

CHAPTER EIGHT
ENTERTAINERS, ARTISTS, SCIENTISTS, EDUCATORS AND LEADERS WEIGH IN

Will Rogers

From Beverly Hills, California:

Dear Bill Durant,

Am I too late -- if I thought of something? Course I haven't thought of anything along the Philosophy line yet, but you can never tell what queer things a man might think of during this depression, they say Hunger produces the best that's in a man, so if this keeps up, something awful good ought to come out of some of us.

I had a little junk in a weekly article, that I already sold once and should give you most of the check for you furnished the idea, If there was anything in there any good to you take it, for a Sunday Syndicated Article is known to never be read, and if so its by somebody that cant remember 24 hours. There was one or two lines in there that might a been cuckoo enough to have been called 'Philosophy.'

When you come out this way, I want to see you and have a chat with you, have you visit me, you would be quite a Curio around these Movie lots -- they got a great slant on life. Well good luck to you, there seems to be no way to keep people from writing books.

Yours,

Will Rogers

I have been stealing so much first-class material from first-rate men who answered my query as to the meaning of life, and the possible destruction of human hope by human knowledge, that I am comforted in my larceny by observing with what sly alchemy the Philosopher of Beverly Hills turns my lead into gold. But being the better thief of the two, I propose to snatch from Will's article (with acknowledgments to the *New York American*) a bit or two of his genial thought:

I guess I just get the usual amount of mail of anyone that

writes junk for the papers, mostly people that sho' don't agree with anything you said in the papers, and showing you where you ought to be calling Hogs somewhere.

But this week I got some interesting letters. One I sure was surprised to get was from Will Durant, a man that has studied philosophy like Mr. Coolidge has politics, and both have reached the height in their chosen professions . . .He wanted me to write him and give him my version of 'What your Philosophy of life is ?' . . .I think what he is trying to get at in plain words (leaving all the Philosophy out) is just how much better off, after all, is an highly educated man than a dumb one? So that's how I figure is the way I got in that list. He knew that I was just as happy and contented as if I knew something, and he wanted to get the 'Dumb' angle, as well as the highbrow.

That education is sorter like a growing town. They get all excited when they start to get an increase, and they set a civic slogan of "Fifty Thousand by the End of Next Year." Well, that's the Guy that sets a College education his Goal. Then when they get the fifty thousand they want to go on to make it a hundred. And the Educated Guy? He is the same. He finds when he gets his post graduate course that all the other Professors have got one, too, and lots of 'em a half dozen. He begins to wonder if he hasn't spent all this time wondering if he knows anything or not. He wishes he had took up some other line. He talks with an old, broad-minded man of the world of experience, and he feels lost. So I guess he gets to wondering what education really is, after all. For there is nothing so stupid as an educated man, if you get off the thing that he was educated in....

The whole thing [life] is a 'Racket,' so get a few laughs, do the best you can, take nothing serious, for nothing is certainly depending on this generation. Each one lives in spite of the previous one and not because of it. And don't start "seeking knowledge," for the more you seek the nearer the "Booby Hatch" you get.

And don't have an ideal to work for. That's like riding towards a Mirage of a lake. When you get there, it ain't there. Believe in something for another World, but don't be too set on what it is, and then you won't start out that life with a disappointment. Live your life so that whenever you lose, you are ahead.

Dr. Charles H. Mayo

We need Will Rogers' good cheer here, for the next reply to

our letter is from Dr. Charles H. Mayo of Rochester, Minnesota, the most famous of American surgeons, who says very briefly:

My dear Mr. Durant:

I think you have summed up in an entrancing way the life of man on earth up to the present time....I am so busy with my work -- and there seems always to be more rather than less -- that I do not find time to write. However, I shall be delighted to read what you write on the subject and shall look for some advice as to how we can be raised above human insects.

With all good wishes,
Sincerely yours,

Charles H. Mayo

Ossip Gabrilowitsch

And a pessimism quite as profound marks the beautifully-written response of Ossip Gabrilowitsch, gracious aristocrat of the piano, who has so often lifted me out of my little self into that mystic ocean of reality which only music reveals:

My dear Mr. Durant:

On my return from a trip abroad I had the pleasant surprise of finding your letter awaiting me. I sincerely wish I could send the reply you desire, inspired by hopeful, constructive convictions. In all honesty, however, I cannot do this. As I study the march of the human race through the centuries and try to understand its present status, I am unable to discern any plan leading to a higher fruition here or elsewhere. Cruelty, injustice, lawlessness seem to characterize the nature and actions of man today as much (though possibly in a different form) as they did thousands of years ago. A glance at the unprecedented chaos -- political, social and economic -- which prevails in the world at present, teaches us this lesson. It is but the inevitable result of our incurable inability or unwillingness to learn by experience; our lack of generosity, our lack of moral courage -- all things as characteristic of the human race today as centuries ago.
Yet love and beauty do exist and humanity is not without

ideals, even if the latter are sacrificed every day, nay every hour, in the foolish quest after material things. One of the questions in your letter to me was: "Tell us where you find your consolation and your happiness, where in the last resort your treasure lies." My personal happiness I find in two things -- art and my family. But will future generations still be in possession of these treasures? That is the question! The beauty of art (as I understand beauty) is being systematically destroyed before our eyes, and cheap sensationalism substituted. Those who would be the prophets of a new art preach to us that beauty is no longer necessarily art's prime object. As for the future of the family, your letter expresses serious apprehension, and I fully share it. The dawn of an industrial revolution has arisen in the East, and if it should sweep the world it may destroy the home, as it has annihilated so many things which heretofore we thought indestructible.

This, my dear Mr. Durant, is not a satisfactory reply to your query.... People generally are unable to comprehend anyone's pessimistic philosophy without suspecting him of a personal quarrel with Fate. Even a great thinker like Schopenhauer did not escape the accusation. How could I? Yet I personally have no complaint to make, I have fared well at the hands of Destiny.

I have always believed, (and I still do) that a man's philosophy of life should be founded not on individual experience but on wide and unbiased observation. We all have eyes to see and ears to hear. The opportunity is given us of watching hundreds of lives besides our own. Should anyone be so narrow as to judge the world by what happens to be his personal good fortune or ill-luck? Because I eat three meals a day, does it follow that there is no starvation anywhere? Because some of us enjoy good health, must we remain blind to the fact that thousands of human beings daily endure the agony of bodily suffering?

Sincerely Yours,

Ossip Gabrilowitsch

This is a fresh breath of honesty from a soul as sensitive as only a musician can be.

Vilhjalmur Stefansson

A different sort of honesty -- bluff and rough like an Arctic wind -- is in the reply of Vilhjalmur Stefansson, who knows life from pole to pole:

Dear Durant:

You ask the expression of a series of personal opinions: *"What help, if any, does religion give in life?"* -- Since the days when I studied religions and philosophy at the Harvard Divinity School, I have given thought to this, but perhaps observation is more important. I have found that religious persons consider themselves better off than if they were irreligious and that irreligious persons consider themselves better off than if they were religious. I have formed no conviction as to which, if either, is right. Personally I never felt inclined to take either religion or alcohol in the hope of drowning sorrow.

"What keeps me going?" -- I suppose it is food, or perhaps rather fuel. For we are essentially heat engines that run according to the quantity and quality of the fuel till some part of the machine gives way.

"What are the sources of my inspiration?" -- Again, food, and the way the body handles it. For instance, two years ago I lived a year in and around New York on exclusively meat and water. During that time I was noticeably more optimistic, looked forward to the next day and the next year with more relish than when on the ordinary mixed diet. Other sources of inspiration are weather, sound sleep. But perhaps, being a philosopher, you want to insist on spiritual inspirations. There are such. My chief one is the feeling that if anything is worthwhile it may be the increase and diffusion of knowledge. So I keep working away at that when convenient. It is not clear that absorbing knowledge from universities and Sunday supplements has taken away from me any more than it has given in return. If no one has found a meaning for life, neither has anyone demonstrated that life has no meaning. What probably is meaningless is the question as to whether life has a meaning.

Vilhjalmur Stefansson

Arther Schnitzler, H. G. Wells, Eugene O'Neill and Havelock Ellis

Some answers were lazy, and referred me to the writer's books. Arthur Schnitzler, shortly before his death, sent on a whole *Buch der Spruche und Bedenken* as his reply; H. G. Wells wearily pointed to all his books as his attempt to meet the issue; Eugene O'Neill wrote that he had tried to face the problem in his trilogy, *Mourning Becomes Electra*; and Havelock Ellis wrote:

Dear Mr. Durant,

The questions you propounded are, of course, the most important that can be asked. All those of us who are really alive spend our lives in answering them and in expressing those answers in our work, whatever shape that work may take.

If you ask me for the briefest and most leisurely statement of my own answers, I would without hesitation name *The Dance of Life*, slowly written during the most mature years of my life. I would add, as dealing with the same question -- though in a way both more intimately personal and more fragmentary -- the three Series of my *Impressions and Comments*, now collected in one volume under the title of *Fountain of Life*.

Sincerely Yours,

Havelock Ellis

Henry Fairfield Osborn

Henry Fairfield Osborn, of the American Museum of Natural History, wrote that his life was too crowded to permit of his discussing its meaning; but he added that "lines of research which I am now carrying on convince me that we must restore the word 'creative' to the word 'evolution,' as distinguished from the old world 'created'"; and named these researches as the central significance and spiritual basis of his life.

Admiral Byrd

Admiral Byrd seems to have struggled heroically with the question, and then given it up as worse than the South Pole: a first response said: "I am interested in your letter.... Undoubtedly the truth is bringing pessimism and despair to many who think. I have given the very problem you bring up a great deal of thought. . . . It isn't impossible that unless some constructive thought is given to the world, despair will do great damage." But meanwhile the man who made short work of geographic mysteries which centuries had failed to solve was caught in the lure of action and pleaded, in a later letter, the inadequacy of time; it was as if life would teach, by this very example, that action is healthier than thought. Sovitur ambulando: even philosophical questions can be answered only by doing things. All thought that does not lead to action, said Goethe, is a disease.

Carl Laemmle

There is another man of action, Carl Laemmle, submerged in the chaos and speed of a motion-picture studio; a man who must deal in action in order to make his pictures live; it would be interesting to know how such a mind faces our problem. Carl Laemmle faces it with the simplicity and candor of a modest man:

Dear Mr. Durant:

I enjoyed your letter, ... and I am glad to answer your questions, but I am sorry to say I am going to disappoint you because my answers, while truthful, will be utterly bromidic. At least that is how I fear they will impress a mind like yours.

If science and philosophy have brought us to the dreadful pass you describe in your letter it doesn't speak very well for too much thought, does it? In my experience, I have found that most of the people I consider slightly off their base are merely victims of too much introspection.

You ask me *"what keeps me going?"* -- My answer is the answer which all smart alecks laugh at -- it is work. I get a tremendous kick out of seeing my ideas take form and bring concrete results. The fact that countless ideas do not work out does not take away from the pleasure I derive from those that do. I like the feel of power -- you see I am being as frank as I know how -- and I like to make a money profit on my work. But the thing that keeps me going is the work itself and the sense of achievement. I cannot play as much as some men do because my eyes are not very good and my hearing is not of the best. So my play consists of a small game of poker with congenial friends, or perhaps a small bet on a horse race.

As for religion, I do not know how much help it gives me.

Very likely it helps me unconsciously and it certainly must have had something to do with the formation of my ideals. Probably, too, it has much to do with my energy although I have no tangible proof of it unless you consider one occasion when I was given up for dead and something pulled me through.

My children, my one grandchild, my other relatives and my friends are my consolations and my happiness. You ask, *"where in the last resort my treasure lies?"* -- I think it lies in an almost frenzied desire to see my children and my children's children well cared for and happy.

I wonder if you had your tongue in your cheek when you said *"we are driven to conclude that the greatest mistake in human history was the discovery of the truth"* -- When was this discovery made? I have not seen any headlines about it in the daily papers. I have supposed that each individual among us was still hoping to make the discovery in his own way and that this hope constituted a large part of his life, whether he was aware of it or not. The truth which different men think they have discovered is probably not the truth at all, and that it why it has not made us free. I still have my delusions -- thank God! -- and I feel sorry for the scientists and philosophers who have thought themselves into a deep pit.

One of the things I am most grateful for is the fact that through a life of hard work, of one menacing crisis after another, of one disappointment and one triumph after another, I still remain an optimist. I do not know just what my main goal is -- other than what I have described -- but I know I would have no goal at all if I were not an optimist.

I would rather remain a hard working businessman and be as happy as I am than become the world's greatest sage and accept all the sourness and hopelessness which seem to go with too much abstract thinking.

Sincerely Yours,

Carl Laemmle

This is how the problem works out in life; we are too busy living to bother much about ultimate meanings; the obligation to get work done puts a cloture on thought. The man with a family to feed has no time for conscious philosophy; if he had he might say that the meaning of life was to feed one's family; and it would be hard to better that answer.

Ernest M. Hopkins

And now look at the problem through the eyes of then President of Dartmouth College --a man of the highest repute among those who know his field. Here again we shall find a healthy distrust of thinking divorced from life:

Dear Mr. Durant:

I have read your letter of June 16 with great care and have with much seriousness considered the questions which you ask. I don't know that in the haste of the post-Commencement season I can give you any statement that will be helpful to you or that will be a sufficiently lucid expression to indicate what I really feel. However, here is my attempt to do what you have asked me to do.

The worth of human life seems to me to be in the opportunity it offers to be. I cannot imagine anyone's questioning the worthwhileness of life, for instance, if an occasional day like this is available to him: Great expanses of blue sky; lazily drifting fleecy clouds; a perfect temperature; a wealth of verdure in trees and shrubs and lawns; the glorious colors of the gardens; and the sounds I heard at daybreak of all sorts of singing birds: these are all experiences beyond measure of value but all sufficient, it seems to me, to give to any normal mind a sentiment that it is a glorious privilege to be alive. Neither scientific analysis nor a multitude of words will describe the reason for the pleasure in the note of a violin string or the song of the white-throated sparrow, but these are not less real because they cannot be analyzed, diagnosed, and explained. For me, therefore, being, with its concomitants of abilities to feel, to think, and to do, is an inestimable boon that life offers and not simply a justification for it to be endured....

The whole modern civilized world of thought has fallen subject to the fallacy that truth is an end in itself rather than that it is simply a means to an end. The approach to fullness of life is along the way of truth, but the path is not the destination. The enduring value of religion is in its challenge to aspiration and hope in the mind of man. The barrenness of much called philosophy is in its tendency to become dialectic, and to ascribe values to words which at best are inaccurate representations of thought without regard to the value of feelings. Feelings are not necessarily untrue because they cannot be expressed. Every great religious leader has in one way or another declared in substance what Jesus said: that he was come to give life, and to give it more abundantly. The philosopher has given no such assurance. He not infrequently has committed himself to an intellectualism sterile of any emotional urge and denying any sufficient goal toward which life might press.

The incapacity of philosophy to reign and rule seems to me to have been its obliviousness to human experience. It has herein failed to check the validity of its intellectual processes. Plato in his familiar passage on philosophers and kings long ago indicated the insufficiency of either thinking or doing as a specialized activity when one was separated from the other: "Until ... those commoner natures who pursue either to the exclusion of the other, are compelled to stand aside ... then only will this, our state, have possibility of life and behold the light of day." . . .

Yours Very Sincerely,

Ernest M. Hopkins

Adolph Ochs

Evidently religion does not die; in the vast majority of men it is still a living force for good and ill. I find a sincere note of it in the reply of Adolph Ochs, who was the publisher of that finest achievement in modern journalism, the New York Times; by this letter I was better able to understand the solid, quiet success of this man in making his paper the most respected and the most influential in America without ever catering to the mob:

Dear Mr. Durant:

Your letter is a gem. I wish you would permit me to publish it. You ask me what meaning life has for me, what help--if any -- religion gives me, what keeps me going, what are the sources of my inspiration and my energy, what is the goal or motive-force of my toil, where I find my consolation and my happiness, where in the last resort my treasure lies.

To make myself clearly understood, if I were able to do so, would take more time and thought than I can give the matter now. Suffice it for me to say that I inherited good health and sound moral principles; I found pleasure in work that came to my hand and in doing it conscientiously; I found joy and satisfaction in being helpful to my parents and others, and in thus making my life worthwhile found happiness and consolation. My Jewish home life and religion gave me a spiritual uplift and a sense of responsibility to my subconscious better self -- which I think is the God within me, the Unknowable, the Inexplicable. This makes me believe I am more than an animal, and that this life cannot be the end of our spiritual nature.

Yours Faithfully,

Adolph S. Ochs

More and more it stands out that a man must combine action with thought in order to lead a life that shall have unity and significance. Surely a monument like the *Times* is meaning enough for one life!

Jawaharlal Nehru

Let us now cross the seas to India, and look at the young rebel who stands next only to Gandhi in leading the struggle of India for liberty -- Jawaharlal Nehru, who became the protagonist of India when Gandhi passed away:

Dear Mr. Durant,

Your letter raises fascinating questions -- fascinating and yet rather terrible. For your argument leads to the inevitable conclusion that all life is futile and all human endeavor worse than useless. You have done me the honor of putting these questions to me, but I feel my utter incompetence to answer them. Even if I had the time and leisure, which unhappily I have not at present, I would find it difficult enough to deal with the problems you have raised.

Indians are supposed to find pleasure in metaphysics but I have deliberately kept aloof from them, as I found long ago that they only confused me and brought me no solace or guidance for future action. Religion in its limited sense did not appeal to me. I dabbled a little in the various sciences, as a dilettante might, and found some pleasure in them and my horizon seemed to widen. But still I drifted and doubted and was somewhat cynical. Vague ideals possessed me, socialistic and nationalistic, and gradually they seemed to combine and I grew to desire the freedom of India passionately, and the freedom of India signified to me not national freedom only, but the relief of the millions of her men and women from suffering and exploitation. And India became a symbol of the suffering of all the exploited in the world and I sought to make of my intense nationalism an internationalism which included in its fold all the nations and peoples that were being exploited.

I was troubled by these feelings and felt my helplessness. These seemed to be no obvious way of realizing my heart's desire. Then came Mr. Gandhi and pointed a way which seemed to promise results, or at any rate which was a way worth trying and afforded an outlet for my pent up feeling. I plunged in, and I discovered that I had at last found what I had long sought. It was in action that I found this -- action on behalf of a great cause which I held dear. Ever since then I have used all my strength in battling for this cause and the recompense I have had has strengthened me, for the reward has been a fuller life with a new meaning and a purpose to it.

This is hardly an answer to your question. But not being a philosopher, but just a man who feels at home in action, I cannot give you a very logical or scientific answer. I have believed in science and logic and reason, and I believe in them still, but at times they seem to lack something, and life seems to be governed by other and stronger forces --instinct or an irresistible drive towards something -- which for the moment does not appear to fit in with science or logic as we know them. History with its record of failure, the persistence of evil in spite of all the great men and great deeds of the past, the present breakdown of civilization and its old time ideals, and the dangers that lurk in the future, make me despair sometimes. But in spite of all this I have a feeling that the future is full of hope for humanity and for my country and the fight for freedom that we are waging in India is bringing us nearer the realization of this hope.

Do not ask me to justify this feeling that I have for I can give you no sufficient reasons. I can only tell you that I have found mental equilibrium and strength and inspiration in the thought that I am doing my bit for a mighty cause and that my labor cannot be in vain. I work for results, of course. I want to go rapidly towards my objective. But fundamentally even the results of action do not worry me so much. Action itself, so long as I am convinced that it is *right* action, gives me satisfaction.

In my general outlook on life I am a socialist and it is a socialist order that I should like to see established in India and the world. What will happen when the world becomes perfect I do not know and I do not very much care. The problem does not arise today. There is quite enough to be done now and that is enough for me. Whether the world will ever become perfect, or even much better than it is today, I shall not venture to answer. But because I hope and believe that something can be done to better it, I continue to act.

I am afraid I have avoided your principal question -- what is the meaning or worth of human life? I cannot answer it except by telling you how I have looked upon life and what motives have driven me to action.

Sincerely yours,

Jawaharlal Nehru

It is a noble spirit that speaks here; the moral idealism of mankind burns more brightly in India than perhaps anywhere else on our earth today. To have a great purpose to work for, a purpose larger than ourselves, is one of the secrets of making life significant; for then the meaning and worth of the individual overflow his personal borders, and survive his death.

C. V. Raman

Hear the same fine aspiration in this letter from another Hindu, the winner of the 1930 Nobel prize for physics:

Dear Mr. Durant,

I have never believed that life is worth living simply for the moment's pleasure or tomorrow's trivial hope. The mind of man is too feeble an instrument fully to penetrate into the great mystery of this world where we find ourselves; but I have always thought that life would be worth living in order to try and understand a little more of it than we do at present.

The intellectual and scientific impulse has indeed been the mainspring of my life and activities. Religious rituals and dogmas possess no significance for me; but the teachings of Buddha or Christ, if not taken too literally, have a value which I recognize and which I believe time cannot diminish. The desire to labor, to achieve and to help others to do likewise, these are the motive powers which have kept me going. I find self-control and not self-indulgence to be the real source of happiness. In the last resort, to win a victory over oneself is a greater thing than conquering the whole world.

With kind regards, I am,
Yours Sincerely,

C.V. Raman

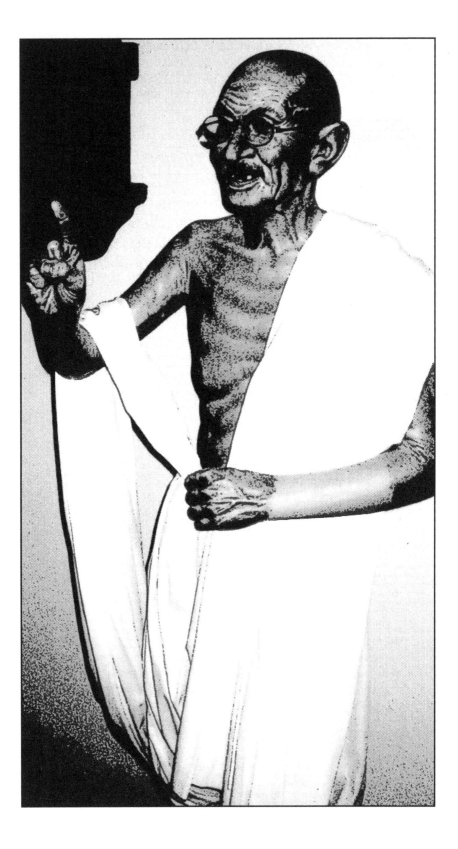

CHAPTER NINE
THE RELIGIONISTS ANSWER

Mohandas K. Gandhi

And now I come to the man who perhaps more than any other on earth personified the power of religion, both to mold the individual and to move the mass. Shortly before leaving for the Round Table Conference in London, Mohandas Gandhi sent the following reply to my query. The omission of personal passages mangles the letter:

Dear Friend,

Your letter of 5th June... Now for your questions.

1. Life for me is real as I believe it to be a spark of the Divine.
2. Religion not in the conventional but in the broadest sense helps me to have a glimpse of the Divine essence. This glimpse is impossible without full development of the moral sense. Hence religion and morality are, for me, synonymous terms.
3. Striving for full realization keeps me going.
4. This strife is the source of whatever inspiration and energy I possess.
5. The goal is already stated.
6. My consolation and my happiness are to be found in service of all that lives, because the Divine essence is the sum total of all life.
7. My treasure lies in battling against darkness and all forces of evil.

You have asked me to write at leisure and at length if I can. Unfortunately I have no leisure and therefore writing at length is an impossibility.

Yours Sincerely,

M.K. Gandhi

This is not quite satisfactory, though we should be grateful to get so much of an answer to our question from a man with a sub-continent on his head, and laboring for the liberation Of 320,000,000 men. The religion that Gandhi here professes seems so different from the more anthropomorphic faith of the hymns which he sang at Sabarmati before the rising of the sun; and there is no word here about that future life which in Hinduism as in Christianity so obsesses the minds of men. Surely the orthodox Brahmins and devout Jains who looked to him as their leader and saint would have been a little disturbed to see how modernistic and modest was Gandhi's theology.

John Haynes Holmes

The same moderate demands on credulity mark the reply of the man who first discovered Gandhi for America -- John Haynes Holmes, then pastor of that magnificent institution, the Community Church of New York. Mr. Holmes writes:

Dear Mr. Durant,

What keeps me going? -- Something within me that burns like a consuming flame when I see falsehood, hypocrisy, injustice, and evil-doing; something without me that pulls like the attraction of love when I catch a glimpse of what this world might be, and may yet be if we try hard enough.

There was a time when I expected to accomplish something before I died -- to see this world changed somewhat because of what I said or did. I cherish this individual expectation as little now as I do the cosmic expectation that this planet will endure beyond a few more million years. No, my eyes will close some day upon the same world upon which they first opened, just as in due time the world itself will end as it began. But meanwhile the universal creative Life has been moving on like a river to some far end unseen, undreamed of, and my life -- not a bit of debris but a constituent drop in the great flood -- has been bending its impulse to the onward sweep of mystic destiny.

I think it is the sense of my creative capacity, matching however microscopically the creative capacity at the heart of the universe, that gives me strength to live -- and great good cheer in the business, too! I try to think when I have felt most happy because most alive. Surely, in the experience of love; surely, also, in hours of crisis, when I have cast all on some great hazard; again, in some swift moment when a "concourse of sweet sounds" in symphony or opera has caught my soul and taught me to relive the emotion of the composer in his original conception; again, when I have myself conceived, in a sudden instant, some vision of the spirit and seen it clothe itself in words upon my startled lips; still again, when I have thrown myself into some cause of justice and the right, and fought to victory or defeat; most of all, perhaps, when I have prayed, or tried to pray, and heard faintly within myself some answer. These are all experiences of creation -- of action that brings order out of chaos and beauty out of order, and thus, within its compass, "makes all things new." It is in such instants that I have felt life in its raw state, so to speak, and therewith, I believe, seen God.

It is this that keeps me going -- the knowledge, vouchsafed in passing moments when we are lifted beyond and above ourselves, that we are an essential part of a creative process -- that we ourselves, with God, are creators, and thus makers of some great cosmic future. What if I cannot see that future, or even imagine it! Such ignorance, frankly confessed, fades like darkness before light in the actual sense-experience of having lived to "vaster issues."

John Haynes Holmes

Abbe Dimnet

But to me, still strangely drawn to the faith of my youth -- loving its beauty while doubting its truth, and wondering whether beauty is not truer than truth -- the most appealing expression of the religious attitude came from the urbane author of *The Art of Thinking*, Abbe Dimnet. His letter is long, but perhaps it will interest the reader as much as it interested me:

Dear Dr. Durant,

Your letter reminds me of a poem of Ch. M. Guerin, which you may know. It begins with these two lines:

Quoique mort a la foi qui m'assurait de Dieu
Je regrette toujours la volupte de croire.

(Though dead to the faith that assured me of God,
I mourn to the end the delights of belief.)

The French poet does not psychoanalyze himself as you do but, in the deeper strata of his consciousness, he seems to see the channels which will some day take him back to the fountainhead of his early belief. Dead to faith, you, too, still crave the comfort of believing, and the pathos which Guerin's rhythm imparts to his stanzas you achieve by the urgent questions quickly succeeding one another towards the end of your letter.

Science has been a harsh stepmother to you. Astronomy, geology and biology told you their tale and there was no faith, no hope and no love in it. You built yourself a philosophy on their data and the philosophy might comment on itself in Remy de Gourmont's words - "The horrible thing about looking for truth is that one finds it." After a few years of bitter satisfaction or purely intellectual delight at possessing those data, you have experienced the usual reaction: what is the good of knowing all these disheartening facts? Better never to have learned anything than know that the universe is a battlefield of cruel forces. Better, a thousand times better, to spend one's short life ignoring all this than be depressed or tortured by knowledge. Our ancestors were happier than we are. The less one knows, the happier one is. Primitive man asked no questions to which his imagination or his sense of harmony with the environing world could not give an immediate answer. He did not exhaust himself by analysis, he just lived and the experience of each minute was enough for him -- a blessed condition which intellectual enjoyment, even of a supreme nature, can never hope to rival. Feeling this you appeal to people whom you suppose to have been nearer to life than yourself and you ask them "what has kept them going, what their source of inspiration has been, what is the goal of their toil, where, in the last resort, their treasure lies."

Your confession invites another, and there is no reason why it should be withheld. I belong to a generation which took even more pride than your own in being scientific and ruled by facts. It certainly has been my privilege to spend the best part of my life in a Parisian sect of learning, the atmosphere of which had nothing in common with what the world generally connotes with the name of Paris. In the shade of our ancient elms and whitewashed walls, we lived the life of a hundred years ago: we were, or tried to be, Parisian in culture, but our effort was constantly refreshed by contact with provincial honesty and provincial simplicity. Many a time a matter-of-fact conversation with the parents of some student would conjure up the turrets and gables of a manor-house in Perigord or the library of a Grenoble magistrate. The virtues of old France were in the background and, as you say, the necessities of life pressed us on all sides -- a blessing, no doubt; one for which I can never be grateful enough.

But our minds were stocked very much as your own is. We were Sorbonne-nurtured; our teachers had been friends of Taine or disciples of Comte. We all dabbled in science and

toyed with philosophy -- I mean the philosophy of the obser-
vatory and laboratory, not that of the Schools with which we
never became acquainted till after we had been introduced to
the philosophers. Philosophy was unsatisfactory, of course.
What can it do in the presence of mysteries except deepen
our sense of mystery? Creation, the beginnings of life, the
dawn of consciousness, the appearance of vision, mind and
reflection remained inexplicable by philosophy as well as by
science. Philosophy's conjectures were inadequate, but how
inadequate science's facts also were! And how conflicting
science's hypotheses! How unexpectedly influenced by pragmatism, too! How could we help noticing that, after the war of
1870, Taine and Renan suddenly turned conservatives,
teaching restraint, prudence and sobriety instead of their former radicalism? Do we not see the same phenomenon in
America? Cheerful boyish unbelief disports itself in the week-
lies, but the philosophical examination of conscience of the
great searchers leads to quite a different state of mind.

Pragmatism or no, there are two ways of looking at the
so-called facts of science. Mine has been hopeful. There was
a time when neither man nor any visible promise of man
existed on our globe. Towards the end of the Tertiary age, the
miracle happened: billions of forms of life had crowded or dis-
placed one another without any one taking any definite
ascendancy, without any epoch-making change. But, at last,
man appeared, consciousness manifested itself in a thousand ways, science was created, developed itself and finally
took hold of the world in a way I never can sufficiently admire.
Only the germs of this development existed a hundred thousand years ago, none of it could have been anticipated a million years ago. To me the idea is full of possibilities.

Astronomy may tell a disheartening tale now. But why
should we infer that it will be so to the hundredth generation
after us? Why should we not hope that with wider compre-
hension, greater security will also come? You notice how vio-
lently we crave immortality in comparison with the ancient
Hebrews. Why should this notion have taken such momen-
tum if there were no foundation for the hope?

I am afraid you have been a scientist *strictioris observan-
tiae*, a Fundamentalist in science -- hence your pessimism.
You should have been on your guard against incomplete
data, against tentative systems. You should never have
called science "truth" as you seem to do in your letter. Your
scientific certainties bred pessimism; more mistrust would
have saved some hope and there is no hope without an
admixture of faith.

You ask what life has done for me? -- It has given me a
few chances to break way from my natural selfishness and

for this I am deeply grateful. But it has also given me greater intellectual stability. I jibed the first time I saw Comte quoting with approval the *Imitation of Christ* saying that "we cannot hope to understand unless we first believe." Newman's teaching was similar. But how clear the experience of life makes it now that it is so. Today my faith and my reason are mutually compelling -- and that means peace. Shall I tell you? It seems impossible to me that you should not gradually come to the same calm -- if not to the same conclusions. Your letter expresses dissatisfaction too violent to last.

Ernest Dimnet

CHAPTER TEN
THREE WOMEN EXPLAIN

So much for the men. But what does woman think of this strange planet of ours, and her life thereon? I should judge that she has wisely refused to think about it at all. Few of the letters that I have received from women had, it seemed to me, faced the problems stated.

I suspect that woman feels these matters deeply, when she is not absorbed in the task of continuing the race; but she cannot yet find words, or superficial intellectual form, for these secret depths. Would that our enemies, i.e., our wives and sweethearts, would write a book -- about themselves, and honestly! -- what a revelation such a document would be to men!

Mary E. Woolley

The first feminine answer is from Mary E. Woolley, who made Mt. Holyoke College one of the finest of our schools for girls:

> Dear Mr. Durant:
>
> Life grows in meaning as I go on. It has not only more signif- icance but, also, more happiness, fewer moods of depres- sion than when I was a girl. At the basis of this increasing sig- nificance is religion. I think that if it were not for that I could not "go on" for I am more conscious of the suffering of the world, more troubled by it. I cannot quite understand how a human being can face life without a belief in a Supreme Power, a Personality with whom communion can be a real thing. My creed is a simple one, with little theology embodied in it. Jesus Christ is to me the supreme revelation of Love and so of God, and His life an inspiration showing how a human life may be lived in kind if not in degree.
>
> I find "motive force of toil" also in other lives, some that I have known personally, others only historically. The fact that there have been human lives of power and beauty is a stim- ulus to living. My own mother and father have been a part of that stimulus, showing in an inconspicuous way what love can accomplish in a human life.

Another "motive force of toil" I find in the chance to have a part in bringing out the possibilities of other lives. I do not see how one can work for years with young people, as I have done, and be a pessimist! I have seen too many lives develop into something fine and strong.

As for "consolations and happiness" I think that they come all along the way. I am writing on an October morning, in the height of the autumn glory, when just to be alive is inspiration, and when the gray days come and moments of depression, the realization that "God's in His heaven," even though far from feeling that "all's right with the world," gives consolation and happiness. So I come back to religion as that which keeps me going!

Mary E. Woolley

Gina Lombroso

From Italy came an apparently simple, and yet probably fundamental reply. It is from Gina Lombroso, daughter of a great psychologist, wife of a great historian (Gulielmo Ferrero), and authoress and thinker in her own right:

Dear Sir,

Many thanks for your letter. The problem you ask me about is the problem which has worried me as every other human being. The sincere answer I succeeded in giving to myself is that the real reason of being is love. Love which ties us one to the other, while living, which ties us to those who have left us, to our posterity. I perfectly remember that when I was a girl I thought my life was tied indissolubly to that of my father, I thought I was born only to help him, I thought I had to disappear with him. After his death I remained tied in the same way to my husband, to my children. I think that the primordial reason of living is love. Love for the family is the best known and the easiest.

When I had some experience in life the reason of my life has been to synthesize this experience so that as many people as possible could make a use of it. In both cases it is the love which ties one to the other which is the reason of life. Love for the family first (I am a woman!). Love for all those which have some resemblances with us and will pass by the same experiences.

With My Best Regards,

Gina Lombroso

Helen Wills Moody

But by far the most interesting reply from a woman was that of Helen Wills Moody. Her very existence is in itself good reason for living; she has done more than a thousand impresarios of anatomy and millinery to "glorify the American girl"; and the American girl at her best -- or the European girl at her best -- is a sufficient achievement of protoplasm to warrant some faith and pride in life. She wrote almost as well as she played the game of tennis:

Dear Mr. Durant,

A twenty-five-year-old must be cautious about what he (or she) says upon such tremendous subjects as you have named in your letter. One of the signs of youth is the feeling that one has all the philosophy of life neatly pigeon-holed. If this is true, it must be, then, that I am quite old, as I am really not quite certain about anything.

The only thing that I know I really want, is some means of exercising the restlessness which seems to be continually in my heart. Tennis, painting -- almost anything will do. As a child I didn't know what it was, but now I think that I recognize it. It is the reason why I have played tennis so fast and furiously for so many years. It is the reason why I studied diligently when at school and even cried when I did not happen to get a "100" in spelling. It is why I tried so hard to win a Phi Beta Kappa key for scholarship in college, which I did, but would have wept, I know, if I had not.

I hope to Heaven this restlessness, this constant hope of arriving at some degree of perfection is not a peculiar form of conceit. To me, it is Religion. It is a "motive force of toil" (of such "toil" as I have done!). By working steadily on the thing that I like, I can remove from my mind momentary spells of sadness or irritation or anger, and afterwards feel happy and *almost* peaceful.

I hope that this constant restlessness, this wish to be in action and on the way towards attaining some degree of perfection is interwoven with the love of the beautiful. It may even be that they are very closely related. It is difficult for me to find words. I know that in contemplating the beauty of perfection in an art, I seem to be transported to another sphere (more words, but I cannot find the right ones). Music, sculpture and, to the greatest degree, painting. (In speaking of perfection in art I do not mean, of course, smoothness or "slickness" in finish, which is the old-fashioned "perfect.") In coming upon color combinations in art and in nature (never nature "in" art), if I may use a commonplace description, I find that I am unable to swallow; such emotion seems to close in upon me, and that I have a correspondingly violent mental reaction (!!). Perfection and beauty fascinate me in any field, but most of all in art, and there in the abstract sense.

Each one thinks himself unique in his feelings, no doubt, and here I am trying to read into the restlessness of my heart a special significance, when the same thing is to be found, perhaps, in the heart of every other young person of my age living in our restless country.

I do know that I do not wish to conform to rules of Religion that are laid out like so many squares bounded by fences -- that you must go here, that you cannot go there. I loathe the Form of Religion. And I know that I would hate life if I were deprived of the right of trying, hunting, working for some objective within which there lies the beauty of perfection.

In my hall there stands an antique Greek head of a woman in cream-colored marble. She was left me as part of a legacy about a year ago. She is really from Ancient Greece, and, except for several small scars, has escaped the centuries with nose, brows, and chin intact. The head is in profile against a cream-colored wall. It stands on a dark marble pedestal. At different times of day the light changes on the face. Sometimes it is faint, so faint upon her forehead, cheek and nose, that her sensitive head scarcely stands away from the cream wall behind. At other times, the light is bright, and the clear-cut profile with its strong yet delicate chin, and thoughtful brows stand out clearly, dominatingly. The curling tendrils of her hair are followed back along her head by the light, almost to where they meet to form the knot. Her neck is strong and rounded and firm. I like to close my eyes and run my fingers over the contours of her face, and thrill each time in discovering modeling that my eye had not detected. It is almost as if you could not know the message of her face until you closed your eyes, and actually felt it through your finger tips. She came from a collector's gallery, but with her, to me, came no history. I know that she is beautiful and that she is nearly perfect.

When I look at the head I have moments of great pleasure, and it makes me feel all the more keenly my restlessness, my desire for activity which has as its goal some sort of beauty and perfection. For me, life is interesting, entertaining, happy, if only I can have some activity for the restlessness that is in my heart. I want that activity to be careless, never finished, and I would like to have it at almost all times dominating my thoughts. I would like to have "a one-track mind" (not closed, of course, to information, because I would like to know about everything), but I would like to be able to enclose myself on my engine on my one track and close my door like a clam closes his, and rush away towards the horizon and the infinite, or whatever its name is.

You ask "where in the last resort your treasure lies?" and I would answer if I knew, if I were only absolutely certain, and dared, "within myself!" But it is ridiculous for one of twenty-five to say that he thinks he is certain. Perhaps I could give you a more coherent description of what I think of life had I been able to absorb the year and a half of philosophy that I had at college. Although I took many notes, and made elaborate outlines with headings, sub-headings, and so on, I somehow missed the point.

A young author who had just won the Guggenheim Prize for his first novel, who was full of enthusiasm about life in general, told me a story last spring in Paris which made me decide that I would have another try at Philosophy. The story was about a Philosopher named Santayana. Upon hearing the name, I remembered having read several books by him at college. (I had vaguely believed him to be some philosopher of the Far East -- with that name. But it seems not. In fact he seems to have been a human being who was once at Harvard!)

This is the story: It was Spring. The warm sunshine and soft breezes were trying to lure students away from their classes. Santayana was seated at his desk reading to his students. His listeners were sitting, or reclining, in various attitudes of inattention. Santayana's voice trailed off, his eyes traveled over his students, and fixed themselves on a tree which grew outside the window. Its leaves were small and tender, and of the green green of new leaves. Santayana closed the book. A short silence elapsed. He rose, and said: "Gentlemen, it is Spring!" He took his hat and never returned.

I hope this story is true. I hope he went away, got on his one track, and has been going along happily ever since. He is (I imagine) in his restlessness seeking something, something which will explain beauty and perfection. He derives his joy (I imagine) from the ceaseless activity which goes with the quest.

No doubt (at least, I imagine) the sculptor who formed my Greek head out of marble had in his heart this restlessness, this desire to search for perfection and beauty. He derived pleasure from his work. It may have been that his greatest happiness came to him on the days when he was chiseling out of marble the contours of this lovely face. That was hundreds of years ago. Today I am thrilled, as I go down my hallway, in seeing this Greek head, and understanding (I think) its message. The message of the restless heart.

I want to be restless, I want always to be in action, and to be trying for some kind of beauty and perfection. Even if I may be lacking in talent, I shall have the pleasure of action - - and there is always Hope -- at least in a young, restless heart.

The other people that you have written to, will have clearly expressed answers to give you. I wish that I had. I wish I could see George Bernard Shaw's. He once told me that tennis should be played in a meadow, with grass a foot high, and with no balls. At least, what I have told you is what I truly believe!!

You must keep in mind several things when you judge my letter -- one, that I am the youngest on your list, and two, that I am the only one who got on your list through *brawn* and not brain!

Most Sincerely,

Helen Wills Moody

P.S. I have concluded that restlessness is a disease. I didn't say much about tennis because it comes under the heading "activity because of restlessness."

P.S.S. If I have enough paint, a large studio, good light (there are always thousands of things to paint) then I am so happy in the activity of painting that I do not care about what astronomers predict, biologists declare, or what Love is said to be or what has happened to Religion. I am sure that I am hatefully selfish.

CHAPTER ELEVEN
THOUGHTS FROM PRISON

Owen C. Middleton: Life-Term Convict 79206, Sing Sing Prison, New York

It occurred to the publishers to send a copy of the initial letter to a man recently sentenced to life imprisonment as a fourth offender; what meaning did life seem to have from the viewpoint of one so unjustly condemned to apparently so empty a future?

The reply was so well thought out, and so well expressed, that it commanded a place in this symposium. I found it incredible that we should have been unable to find any better use for such intelligence than to lock it up forever.

An eminent author and philosopher seeks an answer to that age-old question: What is the meaning or worth of human life? An equally eminent publisher asked me how I manage to bear it in my present position.

To the philosopher, I -- a man serving a life term behind prison walls -- answer that the meaning life has for me depends upon, and is only limited by, my ability to recognize its great truths and to learn and profit by the lessons they teach me. In short, life is worth just what I am willing to strive to make it worth.

To the publisher, I say that life, even from within prison walls, can be as intensely interesting, as vitally worthwhile as it is to any man on the outside. It all depends upon the faith one has in the soundness of his philosophy.

My philosophy of life is a homely one, compounded of many simple beliefs of which truth is the guiding star. Upon my ability to see life in its true aspect, I depend for that mental equilibrium without which I find myself drifting in a welter of conjecture and contradictory speculation.

"We are driven to conclude," argues the philosopher, "that the greatest mistake in human history was the discovery of truth. It has not made us happy, for it is not beautiful. It has not made us free, except from delusions that comforted us and restraints that preserved us. It has taken from us every reason for existence except the moment's pleasure and tomorrow's trivial hope." If our happiness and our reason for existence depended upon our inherent tendency to seek comfort in delusions, false tradition and superstition, then I could agree. We should be unhappy when truth deprived us of their questionable consolation, but they do not.

Truth is not beautiful, neither is it ugly. Why should it be either? Truth is truth, just as figures are figures. When a man wishes to learn the exact condition of his business affairs, he employs figures and, if these figures reveal a sad state of his affairs, he doesn't condemn them and say that they are unlovely and accuse them of having disillusioned him. Why, then, condemn truth, when it only serves him in this enterprise of life as figures serve him in his commercial enterprises? That idol-worshipping strain in our natures has visioned a figure of Truth draped in royal raiment and, when truth in its humble form, sans drapery, appears to us, we cry, "Disillusionment."

Custom and tradition have caused us to confuse truth with our beliefs. Custom, tradition and our mode of living have led us to believe we cannot be happy, save under certain physical conditions possessed of certain material comforts. This is not truth, it is belief. Truth tells us that happiness is a state of mental contentment. Contentment can be found on a desert island, in a little town, or the tenements of a large city. It can be found in the palaces of the rich or the hovels of the poor.

Confinement in prison doesn't cause unhappiness, else all those who are free would be happy. Poverty doesn't cause it, else the rich all would be happy. Those who live and die in one small town are often as happy, or happier than many who spend their entire lives in travel. I once knew an aged Negro who could not tell the meaning of one letter from that of another, yet he was happier than the college professor for whom he worked. Hindus are happy, so are the Chinese, the Africans, the Spaniards, and the Turks. The North, the South, the East and the West all contain happy persons. There are celebrities who are happy, and there are many happy people living obscure lives. Happiness is neither racial, nor financial, nor social, neither is it geographical. What, then, can it be, and from what deep well does it spring?

Reason tells us that it is a form of mental contentment and -- if this be true -- its logical abode must be within the mind. The mind, so we are told, is capable of rising above matter. Can we be wrong then in assuming that mental contentment may be achieved under any condition, even in prison?

There are some who would have us believe that thought, discovery and invention have revealed life as a rather hopeless venture, and mankind a helpless pawn doomed to go down to defeat and oblivion, and from this gloomy prospect man turns and exclaims, "What's the use?"

Natural history teaches us that in the great scheme of evolution, which is the only true and not comparative progress, certain forms of life, unable to adjust themselves to evolutionary changes, have been entirely blotted out. These were devoid of that constructive instinct we call "invention." Life is in a constant state of change, and the development of thought and invention enables us to adjust ourselves to these changes. In fact our very fitness, our only hope of survival, depends upon the fertility of our inventiveness.

The prehistoric fish, when it developed legs with which to climb from its then native habitat or element, was as much of an inventor as were the Wright brothers. T. S. Eliot draws us a very convincing picture of a chaotic world in *The Waste Land*, but I dare to question the premise upon which he paints his picture. Science, discovery, thought and deduction all tell me that the world is a living symbol of orderliness, that evolution is blind only according to man's standards of blindness, that chaos exists only in the minds of men. Reason will not permit me to see life in any other aspect. To me, life is like a river, moving ever forward. There are eddies and crosscurrents, but the main stream sweeps onward.

Life cannot retrogress, neither can man. He is an integral part of the universe in which he lives, that universe which is ever moving forward to some appointed destiny. That life was accidental is a theory I am willing to accept, but it doesn't follow that it need be meaningless. Any man who has thought deeply enough to arrive at the conclusion that life is without meaning must surely be an intelligent man. Intelligent persons do not do meaningless things, yet these exponents of this doctrine continue to live. I am forced to conclude from this that they do not feel entirely in sympathy with their doctrine. Each time I pick up a newspaper and read of some man committing suicide, I say, "There was a man who truly believed that life was without meaning."

Those who decry the machine age as heralding the decadence of the race, do not stop to consider that manual labor is not a natural but an acquired habit of man. It was a crude means by which primitive man sought to adjust himself, sought to survive, a method for accomplishing those tasks and overcoming those obstacles which life presents. The machine is simply a quicker, more efficient means to the same end: Man's struggle to keep abreast, to survive. Just as man has changed his mode of living, so must he change his thoughts, his habits, and perhaps even his form. Back in the dim eons of time man has made several physical changes, why not in the far-distant future toward which we are traveling? Up from the deeps of the sea to the shallows came life, up from the shallows to the land.

This evening I stood in the prison yard amid other prisoners, with eyes lifted aloft, gazing at that great, beautiful sight, the airship *Los Angeles* as it sailed majestically over our heads. Into my mind came the thought that, just as that prehistoric creature struggled up out of the sea to the land, so is man struggling up from the land into the air. Who dare deny that, some day, up, ever up he will struggle through the great reaches of interstellar space to wrest from it the knowledge which will enable him to lift his life to a plane as high above this, our present one, as it is above that of prehistoric man?

I do not know to what great end Destiny leads us, nor do I care very much. Long before that end, I shall have played my part, spoken my lines, and passed on. How I play that part is all that concerns me. In the knowledge that I am an inalienable part of this great, wonderful, upward movement called life, and that nothing, neither pestilence, nor physical affliction, nor depression -- nor prison -- can take away from me my part, lies my consolation, my inspiration, and my treasure.

Owen C. Middleton

CHAPTER TWELVE
THE SKEPTICS SPEAK

The last group is composed of skeptics. Perhaps we should end with them if only to remind ourselves that in the last resort our question is unanswerable.

Bertrand Russell

First from the Bad Boy of England, scandalizer of all continents, and then the prospective terror of the House of Lords.

> Dear Mr. Durant,
>
> I am sorry to say that at the moment I am so busy as to be convinced that life has no meaning whatever. . . .I do not see that we can judge what would be the result of the discovery of truth, since none has hitherto been discovered.
>
> Yours Sincerely,
>
> Bertrand Russell

Count Hermann Keyserling

Second, and most honest of all, from a man who does not care to add to another writer's royalties:

> Dear Mr. Durant,
>
> It is absolutely impossible to answer such questions as you ask in any serious way in the frame of a letter. Besides, when stating my ideas, I prefer using my own setting to providing material for the book of another author.
>
> Yours Truly,
>
> Count Hermann Keyserling

George Bernard Shaw

And last and shortest, and perhaps wisest, a postal bearing the gigantic head and Tolstoian face of G. B. S., and these pithy words in meticulous, impeccable hand:

How the devil do I know?
Has the question itself any meaning?

G. Bernard Shaw

So we have come to the end of our rope. How shall we answer this villainous and murderous postal? Is it possible to catch the meaning of life without getting outside of it to judge it, or without seeing it as part of a larger whole? And which of us can do that? This is a merry termination of our quest, a disturbing illustration of the old definition of metaphysics as "a search in a dark hole for a rat that is not there."

Shall we then give up the quest? Not at all. Now let us face the matter for ourselves.

PART THREE:
THE AUTHOR REPLIES

CHAPTER THIRTEEN
ON THE MEANING OF LIFE

In 1930 I received several letters, from separate persons, declaring their intention of committing suicide. As far as I know none of the gentlemen who so disturbed me with their tragedies killed himself; but I should attribute this not to the cogency of my arguments (which, as frail intellectual things, must be helpless before emotion or despair) but to the reality of pain. Perhaps there is no will to live, but only a fear of death; just as there is no "social instinct," but only a terror of solitude.

I have brought together here the substance of my correspondence with them, and have added, in passing, some comments on the questions stated in the first chapter of this book.

Letters To A Suicide

Dear Unknown,

I have received the announcement of your prospective suicide, and am impressed by the premises you offer for your violent conclusion. That even the simplest man should kill himself is a sufficient indictment of life to stir the attention of a student of human affairs and the daily procession of suicides is one of the bitterest facts that must be included in an honest philosophy. Otherwise, the death of any one of us is a chronological item of no great import in the eye of Nature; "men must endure their going hence even as their coming hither." What interests me in you is the apparent logic of your despair, the completeness with which you survey all life and knowledge, and find them, like Ecclesiastes, discouraging and vain. I ask you to reason with me for a while, even though I know the story of the policeman, who after many appeals, persuaded the would-be suicide to stop and talk the matter over; in the end, as you will recall, they both jumped off the bridge. It is possible that in discussing with you the value of life I shall be convinced, instead, of the attractiveness of death. I take my chance.

Concessions To Suicide

Let me confess at once that I cannot answer, in any absolute or metaphysical sense, your question as to the meaning of life. I suspect that there is some ultimate significance to everything, though I know that our little minds will never fathom it. For the meaning of anything must lie in its relation to some whole of which it is a part; and how could any fragment or moment of life -- like you or me -- pretend to rise out of its individual cell and survey or understand the entirety of things? We play with words like *world* and *life*, *eternity* and *infinite*, *beginning* and *end*, but in our hearts we know that these are only the badges of our ignorance; we shall never understand what they ought to mean. Philosophy, after deposing God, has put man in His place, and endowed man with universal concepts and cosmic perspectives which could properly belong only to a supreme and supernatural intelligence.

Perhaps if we face frankly our mental limitations we shall take even our pessimism more modestly. We shall look upon that gloomy picture of the world which contemporary science paints as one fleeting form in the kaleidoscope of human opinion; we shall remember that there is nothing certain or permanent about that picture, and that the future will probably smile at it as today we smile at Aquinas and Anselm, Scotus and Abelard. Let us not take the astronomers too seriously; they do not know whence our planet came nor whither it is bound, when it began or when it will cease to be; in truth they are as great guessers as the philosophers. As for the geologists, their exuberant cartography of the earth before history is only a charming play of fancy; they cannot be sure of their extinct continents and seas; and perhaps the fossil strata have tumbled themselves about just to deceive these puzzled readers of the rocks. They do not know how old man is, or whether the "ice age" really existed, or whether it put an end to civilization. The physicists do not know what matter is, nor the biologists what life is, nor the psychologists what consciousness is; their brave dogmas are passing emphases on parts or aspects mistaken for wholes. You must not shoot your brains out on the basis of these airy hypotheses; if you do you will join the long list of those holy martyrs who died for absurdities. We must learn to be skeptical even of our scientists.

It seems a little ridiculous to found your despair upon the mechanical philosophy which Spencer has left us as a relic of his mid-Victorian simplicity. While critics and novelists are taking mechanism for granted, the sciences which fought so bravely for it are calling it in doubt, and withdraw in confusion before the complexity and willfulness of the atom and the cell. It is hardly likely that we have personal immortal souls; but it is even less likely that we are machines mechanically mourning our mechanism. Such a philosophy is no reason for suicide; it is reason for a gate of laughter hearty enough to sweep all the dogmas from the infallible vacillating laboratories of the world.

What we can be certain of in science is not its metaphysical assumptions but its physical achievements; the steamship, the airplane, and public sanitation are a little more real than this effervescence of testtubes into philosophy. Take a night flight over New York, and feel the reckless courage and power of these machines called men; accept without apology the thrill of peril and speed; rejoice over the realities of science, and smile at its transcendental theories. There is no knowable limit to what this trousered ape will do with his multiplying discoveries; doubtless he will some day throw his engines around the stars, and deport his criminals to Betelgeuse. If you insist upon dying, undertake tasks of some danger and use in adding to these discoveries; risk yourself in medical or mechanical experiment, and give some significance to your life and death. But whatever you do, don't die of philosophy.

If you pass from science to industry and politics as an invitation to suicide you may find a surer footing from which to catapult yourself into eternity. I grant you that our economic and political life is in chaos, and that if we can invent no better system for organizing the work and government of the world we may as well surrender the earth to another species, or another race. It is true that all government irks us, and that men have been as misruled and discontent under monarchies and aristocracies as under our present democracy of bribes and spoils; and perhaps in our anger at the breakdown of our acquisitive economy in the present century we forget ungratefully its turbulent creativeness in the nineteenth -- no other system had ever produced such wealth or spread such comforts before. But I would not want to cover up with vain optimism these leaking cesspools of our public life; it is better to exaggerate them than to minimize them, provided that we do not let our imperfect perspective sadden and embitter us into a futile despair. Remember that the same greed which has concentrated our wealth so narrowly, and so diminished its purchasing power, lies in our souls too; that the only difference in motive between the rich man and ourselves is seldom a difference in scruples, but is usually a difference in opportunity and skill. In the end we are all guilty together. Let us stop complaining about others, and begin to root the evil out of our own hearts.

The roots of our greed, however, stand so strong and deep in biology and history that we must not expect to eradicate them in a generation -- or a century. Our ancestors gorged themselves when they found food, because they could not know how soon they would find food again; pigs of all species gorge themselves similarly today; and it was in this primitive uncertainty that human greed was born. Our vices were once virtues, necessary in the struggle for existence; they are the tribute which we pay to our origins; we must accept these vestigial relics with a certain equanimity, like our vermiform appendices and our supernumerary glands. Until life is quite secure, and no man need worry about food for himself and those dependent upon him, men will continue to acquire greedily, and to hoard against evil days. Perhaps we shall control this impulse by governmental assurance and regimentation of work and wages for all; or perhaps greed will continue to decrease, as fear has decreased, through the multiplication of wealth and the growth of provision and order.

Meanwhile it is natural that people should be acquisitive, that they should judge men according to their success in winning security, and that nations should rise or fall according to their economic power; in the end, it must be confessed, bread is more important than books, and art is a luxury made possible by wealth. If we see these things in their historical place we shall not tear out our hair, or blow out our brains, because only a majority of our people have food and clothing, shelter and automobiles, schools and libraries, and an equal right with the rich man to imbibe advertisements and saxophones from the air, and murder and adultery from the screen. We shall realize that even in our depression things are better than they were in our youth, and we shall resolve to make them better still for our children.

Is it true that progress is a delusion? Yes, if you mean uninterrupted, general, or everlasting progress. Progress as we know it in history is subject to many setbacks, never moves evenly all along the line (our progress in science and industry is not accompanied now by progress in philosophy and art), and at some distant date, presumably, all its works will be destroyed. But to doubt its reality because of its end would be like calling the sun a delusion because it will set. Even that distant end to progress is a presumption, conceded here out of argumentative generosity; we are not sure of it; and meanwhile there is much evidence for believing that the material, physical and mental status of the average man on the earth today -- bad as that status is -- is higher than it ever was before. Students despair of their own age because they compare the average man of their acquaintance with the exceptional men of the past; let them study a little further, and they will find that not all the Athenians were geniuses, and that not all of these geniuses were saints; they will discover, behind Plato and Aristides, a corrupt democracy, a suppressed womanhood, a superstitious people, and a brutal mob.

States come and go, and civilizations are in great measure lost; but so much of these "dead" cultures remain that if we were to devote a whole lifetime to the task of absorbing even the Greek fraction of our mental heritage we could not possibly encompass it all. Euripides and Aristotle are not dead; Confucius and Lucretius are our contemporaries; even Hammurabi and Ptah-hotep speak to us intelligibly across four thousand years. And our means of preserving, transmitting and disseminating this mounting cultural inheritance of knowledge, morals and arts are more abundant today than in any age of the past.

The most depressing sight in our civilization is not poverty but the apparent deterioration in the moral fiber of the race. It is hard to judge of these things, partly because one's experience is so brief, partly because we judge the morals of today with the standards of yesterday. We forget that these standards were made for an agricultural life, and can have no absolute validity in an industrial and urban age. It is ridiculous to expect the morals of a rural community from men delaying marriage till thirty, and living amid the million contacts, opportunities and stimuli of the city -- other times, other morals. The more I see of men and women the less critical I am of them; they are not half so bad as their newspapers and moving pictures make them out to be; it is because they are prosaically decent that they demand, for the vicarious fulfillment of ancient impulses to polygamy and the chase, that their press and their films shall reek with promiscuity and crime.

Nevertheless a subtle degeneration, not so much in morals as in character, seems to have begun in our people. Through the wisdom of our legislators, only the intelligent may contracept, while the stupid are commanded to reproduce their kind. In result, the educated minority (rich or poor) brings up less than its share of the next generation, the uneducated majority brings up more; in each generation we create by education a brain for our society and then, by the dysgenic effect of our legislation, we cut it off again. The educator is frustrated, and superstition, that *infame* which Voltaire thought he had crushed, flourishes as before, leaving progress to be created and maintained by a precarious and sterile fragment of the race. In this unregulated reproductivity of the mob lies the secret of our political corruption, and the raw material of our municipal "machines"; democracy goes to pieces because "there is always a majority of fools."

Perhaps in this way the old Yankee type, full of independence and grit, is being breeded out, and a new type -- less vigorous in thought and courage -- is taking its place. Our tradition of individual freedom has left the film director and the theatrical producer free to enrich themselves by parading

pornography, recklessly accelerating youthful sex development; and the impulses so precociously aroused find such
mechanical facilities and opportunities for their expression
that our city populations tend to lose themselves at the bottom in crime and at the top in sex. The end product at the top
is a blasé and cynical epicurean who would take to his heels
at the first call of hardship or danger. Nations do not grow
great on such men. We smile at the Puritan today, but it may
be just the virtues of the Puritan that will be needed -- or are
needed now -- when crisis comes: the same stern self-disci-
pline, the same stoic capacity to suffer and persevere, which
made nearly all the strong characters in modern history.

This jolly riot of sex, so pleasant to the individual and so
hazardous to the race, is bound up, no doubt, with the decay
of supernatural belief; and we are engaged at the moment in
a gigantic experiment with the possibility of maintaining social
order and racial vitality through a moral code resting solely on
the earth, and shorn of those supports which once suspend-
ed it from the skies. That experiment failed in Athens, and it
failed in Renaissance Italy. Apparently it is dangerous to the
race to emancipate the individual -- destroy his delusions,
and the villain ceases to breed. This process has already
undermined the leadership of America in literature, morals,
and municipal politics; as it goes on, the same process will
probably weaken all the peoples of Western Europe and
North America. In the interim we shall, in all likelihood, have
a cultural outburst like that of Florence and Rome in the days
of the Medici and the Borgias. In the end we shall be an
extinct volcano, and Asia will mount again the throne of the
world, until it, too, becomes very intelligent and dies.

Mid-Victorian

You will see that I am granting you a great deal -- that life
has no meaning outside of its own terrestrial self, that the
individual has no immortality, and that every civilization, as
surely as every flower, decays. These conclusions seem to
me now so natural that they do not disturb me any more; I
perceive that within the limits set by them I have still much
room to find significance for my life and race, and even a

moderate content. This Byronic pose of our youth, which wished to die because Santa Claus was dead, wears away as the realities of life catch us in their grip and sweep us into action; we find less and less time for mourning idle dreams; and we observe that our children do not pine as we did for myths which they have never believed.

The meaning of life, then, must lie within itself; it must be independent of individual death, even of national decay; it must be sought in life's own instinctive cravings and natural fulfillments. Why, for example, should we ask for an ulterior meaning to vitality and health? They would be goods in their own right, even if they were not also means to racial ends. If you are sick beyond cure I will grant you viaticum, and let you die; let me not to the ending of botched lives put an impediment. But if you are well -- if you can stand on your legs and digest your food -- forget your whining, and shout your gratitude to the sun.

The simplest meaning of life, then, is joy -- the exhilaration of experience itself, of physical well-being; sheer satisfaction of muscle and sense, of palate and ear and eye. If the child is happier than the man it is because it has more body and less soul, and understands that nature comes before philosophy; it asks for no further meaning to its arms and legs than their abounding use. Perhaps if we used our arms and legs we would be happy too; and golf, which God invented for George Babbit, is justified by every mile that is walked and every ball that is lost.

Even if life had no meaning except for its moments of beauty (and we are not sure that it has more), that would be enough; this plodding through the rain, or fighting the wind, or tramping the snow under the sun, or watching the twilight turn into night, is reason a-plenty for loving life. Let death come; meanwhile I have seen the purple hills of South Dakota, and one point of a star taking its place quietly in the evening sky. Nature will destroy me, but she has a right to -- she made me, and burned my senses with a thousand delights; she gave me all that she will take away. How shall I ever thank her sufficiently for these five senses of mine -- these fingers and lips, these eyes and ears, this restless tongue and this gigantic nose?

Love

Do not be so ungrateful about love. To ignore its psychological developments is as unrealistic as to forget its physiological bases. Yes, at bottom it is a matter of hydraulic pressure and chemical irritation; but at the top it becomes, occasionally, a ballade of devotion and chivalry -- -no longer mutual itching, but mutual consideration. I have not in mind here merely romantic love -- that idealization of the object which comes with frustrated desire, and is now disappearing because desire is not so frustrated as before; I refer to the attachment of mates or friends who have gone hand in hand through much hell, some purgatory, and a little heaven, and have been soldered into unity by being burned together in the flame of life. I know that such mates or comrades quarrel regularly, and get upon each other's nerves; but there is ample recompense for that in the unconscious consciousness that someone is interested in you, depends upon you, exaggerates you, and is waiting to meet you at the station. Solitude is worse than war.

I suspect that most pessimists are bachelors; married men have no time for gloom. By a pessimist I do not mean one who has a realistic awareness of the evils and hardships of human life; I mean one who, unable to face those hardships with equanimity, concludes from his own weakness that all life is a worthless snare. Perhaps a good deal of this pessimism comes from thinking of ourselves as individuals -- as complete and separate entities. I note that those who are cooperating parts of a whole do not despond; the despised "yokel" playing ball with his fellows in the lot is happier than these isolated thinkers, who stand aside from the game of life and degenerate through the separation. "Be a whole or join a whole," said Goethe. If we think of ourselves as part of a living (no merely theoretical) group, we shall find life a little fuller, perhaps even more significant. For to give life a meaning one must have a purpose larger than one's self, and more enduring than one's life.

If, as we said at the outset, a thing has significance only through its relation as part to a larger whole, then, though we cannot give a metaphysical and universal meaning to all life in general, we can say of any life in particular that its meaning lies in its relation to something larger than itself. Hence the greater fullness of the married and parental -- as compared with the celibate and sterile -- life; a man feels significant in proportion as he contributes, physically or mentally, to the entity of which he acknowledges himself a part. We who are too superior to belong to groups, who are too wise to marry or too clever to have children, find life empty and vain, and wonder has it any meaning. But ask the father of sons and daughters "What is the meaning of life?" and he will answer you very simply: "Feeding your family." The attraction of the sexes, which, when taken in isolation from its biological function, seems a delusion and a vain pursuit, becomes a road to fulfillment and a modest significance when surrendered to heartily in the continuity of life.

Here on the train from Morgantown to Pittsburgh is a woman all smiles, playing with her child. Oh you unhappy intellectuals of the cities! -- do you think you are profounder than that woman? And you sophist scientist, vainly seeking to understand the part in terms of the part, can you not see that this woman is a greater philosopher than you, because she has forgotten herself as a part, and has found a place in the whole?

A Personal Confession

This, then, I should say, is the road to significance and content: join a whole, and work for it with all your body and mind. The meaning of life lies in the chance it gives us to produce, or to contribute to, something greater than ourselves. It need not be a family; that, so to speak, is the direct and broadest road, which Nature in her blind wisdom has provided for even the simplest soul; it may be any group that can call out all the latent nobility of the individual, and give him a cause to work for that shall not be shattered by his death. It may be some revolutionary association to which a man or a woman gives devotion unstintingly; or it may be a great state to whose preservation and exaltation some Pericles or Akbar devotes his genius and his life. It may occasionally be some work of beauty that absorbs the soul in its making, and becomes a boon to many generations. But in every case it must, if it will give a life meaning, lift the individual out of himself, and make him a cooperating part of a vaster scheme. The secret of significance and content is to have a task which consumes all one's energies, and makes human life a little richer than before.

As for myself -- for I wish to answer directly the questions which I have asked of so many others -- the meaning of life lies perhaps too narrowly in my family and my work; I wish I could boast of consecration to a larger cause. The sources of my energy are egotism and a selfish altruism -- the greed for applause, and a mad devotion to those dependent upon me.

The goal and motive force of my work? -- to see happiness around me, and to win, at last, the approval of my betters. The haunts of happiness? -- my home and my books, my ink and my pen. I would not call myself happy -- no man can be quite happy in the midst of the poverty and suffering that still survive about him today; but I am content, and inexpressibly grateful. Where, in the last resort, does my treasure lie? -- in everything. A man should have many irons in the fire; he should not let his happiness be bound up entirely with his children, or his fame, or his prosperity, or even his health; but he should be able to find nourishment for his content in any one of these, even if all the rest are taken away. My last resort, I think, would be Nature herself; shorn of all other gifts and goods, I should find, I hope, sufficient courage for existence in any mood of field and sky, or, shorn of sight, in some concourse of sweet sounds, or some poet's memory of a day that smiled. All in all, experience is a marvelously rich panorama, from which any sense should be able to draw sustenance for living.

The hardest question of all to answer is: what help does religion give me? As I write the query down I look out of the moving window and see, in the valley below, a little hamlet gathered about a church. I can imagine what incredible theological nonsense is preached under that white spire, what bigotry and sectarianism are nourished there, and with what terror and hatred these simple toilers of the soil will defend the faith that so solicitously protects them from our passing truth. But my heart goes out to them; I think I like them better than the village atheist who knows so well how to say the right thing at the wrong time; to be in haste to destroy the faith of such people is surely the mark of a shallow and ungenerous mind.

Nevertheless, I cannot believe, in the face of biology, in the eternity of the individual self; nor, in the face of history, can I believe in a personal anthropomorphic God. But unlike the tougher minds of my time I miss these encouragements, and cannot quite forget the poetry with which they surrounded my youth. There is something ridiculous in the idea of a Supreme Being that should be at all like a man, even like Leonardo or Goethe; but I should be grateful to anyone who could persuade me of this delectable absurdity. There is something selfish in the desire for personal immortality, and a heaven crowded to suffocation with interminable egos would be an insufferable place; but I suspect that I, too, shall be sorry to go, and should be glad to know, when I am gone, what fate befalls my children and my friends, and the causes I tried to serve.

So that, though the dogmas of the old faith have gone from me and offer me no support today, they have left in me an aroma of their memory, as a certain fragrance may linger in a room from which flowers have been recently removed. So much of the old faith remains that I cannot accept the crude mechanism which contented so many of my generation, and am pleased to find symbolic profundities in the ancient creed. Possibly in the end, faith, ever clamoring to be heard, will break down my doubts, and I shall go the way of Huysmans and Chesterton -- my readers should beware of what I write when I am old.

What immortality means to me now is that we are all parts of a whole, cells in the body of life; that the death of the part is the life of the whole; and that though as individuals we pass away, yet the whole is made forever different by what we have done and been. What God means to me is the First Cause, or source of all life and energy, in which we live and move and have our being; and the Final Cause, or goal and embodiment of our striving and aspiration, that distant perfection which is not but may be. Perhaps that greatest Whole, to which in all generations the greatest souls have devoted themselves, will, in tomorrow's religion, be called God.

An Invitation

But here I have lost myself so much in myself that I have forgotten you, my unknown soldier of despair, who are about to commit suicide. You will see that what you need is not philosophy, but a wife and a child, and hard work. Voltaire once remarked that he might occasionally have killed himself, had he not had so much work on his hands. I notice again that it is only leisurely people who despair. If you can find no work in this chaotic industrial system of ours, go out to the first farmer and ask him to let you be his hired hand for your food and a bed until better things come. If he is afflicted with that incredible disease called overproduction, agree that you will produce only as much as you can consume. Perhaps when we are all permitted to consume as much as we produce we shall have no "overproduction" any more.

In the end I know how vain and snobbish all advice is, and how hard it is for one human being to understand another, but come and spend an hour with me, and I will show you a path through the woods which will better dissuade you from surrender than all the arguments of my books. Come and tell me what a childish optimist I am: lay about you freely, and damn this middling world as you will; I shall agree with everything but your conclusion. Then we shall eat the bread of peace together, and let the prattle of the children restore our youth.

ABOUT THE AUTHOR

Will Durant (1885-1981) was awarded the Pulitzer Prize (1968) and the Medal of Freedom (1977). He spent more than fifty years writing his critically acclaimed series of books entitled *The Story of Civilization* (the later volumes written in conjunction with his wife, Ariel) and capped off his magnificent career with *Heroes of History*, written when Durant was 92. His first book *The Story of Philosophy* has remained in print for over seven decades is credited with introducing more people to the subject of philosophy than any other work. Throughout his life, Durant was passionate in his quest to bring philosophy out of the ivory towers of academia and into the lives of everyday men and women. A champion of human rights issues such as the brotherhood of man and social reform long before such issues were popular, Durant, through his writings, continues to entertain and educate readers the world over, inspiring millions of people to lead lives of greater perspective, understanding and forgiveness.

ABOUT THE EDITOR

John Little is the world's foremost authority on the life, work and philosophy of Will Durant. Little is the only person ever authorized by the Will Durant estate to review and use the entirety of Durant's writings, personal letters, journals and essays. He is the founder and director of the Will Durant Foundation (www.willdurant.com) and has lectured on philosophy in Trinity College, Dublin and the National Museum of Film & Television (England). In addition, he writes books and magazine articles on philosophy, men's health and conditioning and is an award-winning documentary filmmaker.

If you share or would like more information on Will Durant's life-enhancing philosophy, or would like to obtain more writings, as well as audio and video products featuring Will Durant's teachings, we encourage you to visit us at www.willdurant.com.

CPSIA information can be obtained
at www.ICGtesting.com
Printed in the USA
BVHW071648120720
583397BV00002B/131